Girl Power

Get it!

Flaunt it!

Use it!

Caroline Plaisted

Piccadilly Press · London

CAROLINE PLAISTED worked in publishing for fourteen
years before the birth of her daughter in 1994. Since then she has
become a freelance editor and has taken the opportunity to indulge in
writing. Caroline lives in Kent with her husband, two children,
Hannah and Harry, two dogs and two cats. This is her
second book for Piccadilly; the first book is
Enter the Boy-zone: Sport Sorted for Girls.

Printed and bound in Bridgend by WBC for the publishers
Piccadilly Press Ltd, 5 Castle Road, London NW1 8PR

A catalogue record for this book is available
from the British Library

ISBNs:1 85340 488 8 (trade paperback)
1 85340 493 4 (hardback)

Design by Judith Robertson
Cover design by Isobel Smith

Contents

☆

With thanks to Harriet Ashby
for her help and advice

Introduction

SO what is all this about girl power? What *is* girl power? Well, girl power is about you. About you feeling good about yourself and about other people. Girl power helps you do what you want to do, when you want to do it. And the great thing about girl power is that, whether you've already realised it or not, you've already got it. Just take a look at the Spice Girls (OK, OK, so you may think their music is naff but give the girls some credit) – they used their girl power to show what girls are really all about: talent, making the most of their looks, a positive, 'go-get' attitude, the ability to take the world by storm. And, on top of all that, they made the rest of us realise that we have all this too!

This book is all about finding your own girl power and helping you to decide how you want to use it so that you can get the most out of yourself and the most out of life. So get the girl power out, flaunt that girl power – and start using it fast!

1

Girl Power
And How To Get It

REMEMBER when you were about eight and you didn't care what anyone thought about anything? If you felt like wearing a pair of trainers with your best tartan party dress, you just did; make-up wasn't even an issue (unless you went into your mum's room and had a sneaky session with her mascara); boys were, well, just mates like the rest of your mates and you decided that you fancied being an astronaut because you'd like to travel (and no one had yet told you that you would need to get physics A level to be one). Well, bet you didn't realise that when you were eight you had girl power. And that you used to flaunt it and use it all the time – without even realising it. Because girl power is all about confidence, about feeling good about yourself and what you look like and not being restricted by what other people think.

AND NOW you probably feel that you haven't got girl power. Because you've got spots . . . because you haven't got the latest Kookai gear . . . because you haven't got a boyfriend . . . because the boyfriend you've got isn't that good-looking . . . because you don't know if you're going to pass your exams . . . because you think you've got a big bum . . . because you reckon you're not funny enough . . . Well, actually, you are wrong! You have still got girl power, honest. It's just that lately you don't know where you put it. So start asking the right questions so that the answers can reveal where you hid it . . .

Isn't girl power all about being aggressive? I'm not sure that that's what I want to be.

ABSOLUTELY NOT! Girl power is all about confidence and being sure about yourself and what you do. You can be confident and tough by all means, so that you can cope with the knocks you might get in life, but that doesn't mean you have to be rude or antagonistic and go round behaving like some ghastly bully.

THE COMMON REASONS FOR GIRLS TO FEEL POWERLESS

I used to really love sport and played in the school team. But then my best mate said it was taking up too much of my time – time that I should have been spending with her. Now I've given up my sport and hang out with my mate every day after school. The other girls in the team don't really talk to me any more. How can I make friends with them again?

TRY BEING YOURSELF instead of just being an extension of your best mate. OK, so she's lots of fun and stuff – but she's not the only girl out there and you certainly don't have to do everything just to suit her. Girl power is about doing things to suit yourself as well as other people. Does your best mate stop doing the things she wants to do because of you? Shouldn't think so. Having a happy life is all about everything you do being balanced and varied. You can be in the school team and still have plenty of time to see your best mate. And by being in the school team you'll have lots of other friends too, that you can see on the nights when your best mate is off doing what she wants to do. You'll also keep yourself fit and healthy by being sporty. How many couch potatoes do you know that ooze girl power? Take a look at chapter two, Your Image for more thoughts about how to keep looking good so that you keep feeling good. And chapter four, Your Friends talks about how to keep your old mates as well as make new ones.

But how can I look – and feel – cool if I haven't got loads of money to spend on clothes?

THE CLOTHES don't wear you, you know – it's you that wears the clothes. They don't have to be staggeringly expensive either. Or an entirely new outfit every week. If you haven't got much cash in your purse why not think about getting a Saturday job so that you can have some cash to spend on your wardrobe? (Take a look at chapter seven, Getting A Life for ideas about getting a job and earning.) And work out exactly what style of clothes and colours you feel good in all the time. If you feel good, you'll look good. If you look good then you'll be confident – and ooze girl power to your best advantage.

I'll never get a chance to do anything at my school. Nothing ever happens here. It's boring, the teachers are a pain and they don't seem to like me.

TALK yourself into a hole and you'll probably end up stuck in it, girl! OK, so teachers can be a pain but it's extremely unlikely that they don't want you to do well, isn't it? After all, if you do badly in a teacher's lesson then it isn't going to reflect well on them. But if you think they think you are a pain, why do they think this? Could it be because you once did something silly like flood the staffroom when they were all having their coffee break? Or that you lark around in every class?

Getting on with teachers instead of aggravating them actually takes far less energy, making lessons much easier to get through and more fun (yes, I know it may sound unlikely, but they can be fun!). This will help you get more on top of the subject and you'll have a much better chance of doing well. And then the teacher is likely to calm down and may even appear to be a bit more human. The sky's the limit, and if you want something you can have it – but only if you work out how to get it. And what's all this about nothing happening at your school? Of course things happen there – you just need to find out more about them and get involved. Remember, girls with power know how to get information and use it to meet their needs!

Every time I get dressed up for a night out my mum and dad throw a wobbly about my clothes, what time I'll be back, who I'm going out with, where we're going . . . the works! And they usually do it in front of my bloke as well! It's yonks before I can move out and get a place of my own. How can a girl have any power with parents like mine?

NO MATTER how much you love them, parents will always let you down at some stage. At the risk of inducing a great yawn session, remember that the main reason why parents drone on is because they do actually care about you and what's going to happen to you. Also, don't forget that you've died laughing over your dad in his turquoise shell suit on more than one occasion and given your mum a hard time about wearing trousers that are just too tight for that gluteus maximus of hers. Life is about give and take – you need to come to an understanding with your mum and dad so that you can all live happily in the same place, have some privacy – and some fun! Take a look at chapter six, Golden Oldies And Sophisticated Superiors to find out how to cope with *all* the oldies in your life.

All my mates have got really good-looking boyfriends but I've never had one. What am I doing wrong?

NOTHING PROBABLY. It's just that you haven't got round to having a boyfriend yet because you've had plenty of other things to keep you busy. Or because all the boys in your neighbourhood aren't that fanciable. Or because all the boys who are, are already going out with your chums. Stop and think for a minute, though. Are your friends' boyfriends really *all* good-looking? Or do they perhaps just seem that way because you haven't got a boyfriend at the moment? Boys are just an incey wincey part of a girl's life. Girls can have fun *without* boys and having a boyfriend is most definitely not a necessity. But boys do exist, so you'll find out how to get them sorted in chapter five, Boys.

2

Your Image

HOW you look determines how the rest of the world sees you and shows it how you see yourself. Let's take the two extremes of dressing as our starting point:

1 You turn up at a birthday party wearing torn and tatty jeans, a dirty sweatshirt and smelly trainers that have seen very many better days. Your hair is greasy, your glasses have got smears on the lenses and there is dirt under your fingernails. What do you think this image is saying about you? That you are so pleased to be here that you've rushed straight from your previous appointment? Sorry but no. It does not say that. What is says is, 'Actually I didn't dress up because I couldn't be bothered and don't care.' Having said this, perhaps the invitation you received was to a grunge retro party. In which case, you've come in the right gear! But why isn't everyone else wearing it . . . ?

2 You turn up for an autumn geography field trip in a pair of stilettos, a micro mini and no jacket, with hair and nail extensions that Lily Savage would be pleased to boast. What does this tell the others on the trip? Basically that you couldn't have been listening when Miss told you where you were going today because if you had known you would, presumably, have put on your wellies like everyone else and at least packed your parka if not worn it. Girls with power aren't just the doers in life – they are the listeners as well. Just like on page 49, girl power is about listening to things and using the information gained to act in the best way to suit you. Whatever the situation, if you dress inappropriately, you'll be feeling uncomfortable and at a disadvantage. And this field trip is going to be much less hassle if you're wearing wellies and waterproofs! Sure, girls with power want to look good – that's only human – but your clothes should never be a handicap, wasting your time and energy or making you feel pressured and self-conscious.

so you see your image is important to you. If you get it right it makes you feel good about yourself, in control and ready to face anything and (virtually) anyone. The style of clothes you wear is entirely up to you. If you feel comfy in jeans and trousers and positively hate skirts, that's fine. But perhaps you're into minis and stripy tights? Well, that's OK too.

Unfortunately, fashion is a fantastic thing that is perfectly hateful at the same time! You just get around to saving up for the latest gear and then something new arrives on the scene and you are already feeling out-of-date. And there ain't nothing worse than thinking your mates are sniggering about your trousers behind your back, is there? It takes most of us years to work out exactly which style is right for us but, in the meantime, you can do a few simple things to make sure that you look as good as you possibly can, all the time. Girls with power wise up and have a few basic but stylish items in their wardrobe: not least a pair of jeans, a black skirt/trousers and a white shirt that goes with everything. But there are some other things that can help make you look and feel good now . . .

POWER POSTURE

WALK into a room with your head held high and your shoulders back and you will walk in with girl power. Shuffle into the room with your head looking down to your toes and probably no one will notice you . . . OK, so posture may sound like something your gran talks about, but it can work wonders!

Apply posture to your problems

Help! I'm really short, just like my mum and all her sisters. It's awful . . . all the boys call me 'titch' and the teachers make me sit at the front of the class so that I can see the board. I'm not bad-looking but I can't get any decent clothes because all the clothes in the shops swamp me.

OK, so you're not tall enough to make a supermodel. Before you get too fed up with your height, it's worth remembering that some people (OK, so it's only a few people) go through a growth spurt in their late teens and early twenties. If you are a lot shorter than anyone else in your family, it could be that your pituitary gland (which helps to control your growth) has a problem which a doctor could help with. But if most of the people in your family

14

aren't especially tall then there is a good chance that you will follow in their footsteps. However, don't despair! There's a lot you can do to look taller.

First, think taller! Make sure your neck isn't hunched into your shoulders and hold your head high – don't look as if you are apologising for not being a giant. Your hair shouldn't swamp your face – in fact, a shorter haircut can often give the illusion of height. (Ask your hairdresser for advice about this.) Walk with a purposeful stride rather than taking tiny little tippy-toe steps and use platform shoes to your advantage! After all, one of the good things about being shorter is that you almost certainly won't have gigantic feet.

Just like everyone else, *you* should wear your clothes rather than let them wear you. Long skirts and jumpers will only drag your shoulders closer to the ground. If *you* feel good wearing them then why not show a bit of leg and wear shorter skirts and hot pants! Keep jackets and coats short too. Of course, the lucky thing about being smaller is that you can take advantage of all the trendy young teen clothes that lots of the shops sell at cheaper prices (because you don't have to pay the VAT).

Finally, remember that people with big personalities seem like bigger people: Demi Moore may have a giant's image but she certainly has not got a giant's height.

I wish I was shorter like her! I'm taller than everyone else in my school – and I've never come across a boy taller than me, or even the same height as me for that matter. People are always asking me what the birds are doing up in the trees!

DID YOU EVER see Naomi Campbell looking embarrassed about her height? Or Claudia Schiffer? Or any of the other supermodels? No way. Apart from the disadvantage that being taller can make people think that you are older than you are (although, come to think of it, there can be advantages in being thought to be older sometimes . . .) there are loads of things which make being tall great. For a start, people will automatically have a lot more respect for you. And then there are those long, long legs which you've got which look great in trousers, long skirts *and* minis. You can get away with long, luscious locks or a shorter haircut – the choice is yours.

Whatever you do, don't be tempted to hunch your shoulders and slouch in order to seem shorter. Instead of losing inches you will just draw attention to your height and run the risk of making yourself the victim of a bully who can see you aren't feeling full of girl power. So look up, keep your shoulders down and back, and be proud of yourself. Similarly, don't let yourself sink into your hips, round your back and hunch your shoulders up into your neck because it will just make you look slumped and give you a waistline bigger than the one you've actually got!

My gran is always nagging me about the way I sit when I'm watching the telly or doing my homework. She reckons I'm doing myself some permanent damage. I reckon she's just talking a load of gibberish. Surely it doesn't matter how I sit, does it?

WELL it probably depends on how you are actually sitting and how often you sit like it. It certainly isn't a great idea to sit with your legs and feet tucked underneath your posterior for huge amounts of time. It's bad for your circulation and you will also be twisting your spine sideways as well as having to lean more heavily on one elbow. That's probably OK when you're watching the telly for a couple of hours but if you are sitting like this when you are studying then you'll almost certainly be having to hunch your arms and shoulders over the table or desk that you are working at. Then your head will be very close to the page you are reading or writing at which isn't any good for your eyes either!

If you still think your gran's talking a load of garbage (and perhaps you think that this sounds like an answer from your granny!), spare a few moments to consider the posture of the people you come across every day. If you go into the bank and the cashier is slobbing all over the desk, doesn't it make you think 'Is this person slobbing about with my cash too?' And if your teacher is slouching back in his chair with his feet on the desk when you go into his classroom, you probably think 'Whoopee! Two periods of dossing around – this guy won't be bothered!' You see, if your posture oozes girl power then your body language will as well, so people will notice you, take you seriously and know that you mean business!

There's an old bag of a teacher at school who never stops whingeing about me and my mates scuffing our feet. Who cares?

IT'S A REAL BORE when someone nags you about this, but basically it's up to you. Scuffing your heels along the ground is a bit like slouching as opposed to standing up to your full height or sitting straight – if you pick your feet up properly when you walk you'll walk with purpose. You'll look like an energetic person who knows what she's about. A girl with power!

The GIRL POWER Posture Checklist

☆ Be proud of your height whether you're short or tall!

☆ Look up – it'll be more interesting than seeing what's on the ground!

☆ Keep your shoulders back to show off your clothes properly!

☆ Don't cover your face with your hair! However beautiful your locks are, your face looks good too.

☆ Relax – don't let yourself look tense and tortured.

☆ Don't walk as if you are apologising for taking up space on the pavement!

☆ Smile!

YOUR CLOTHES

OK, so you probably haven't got loads of disposable income to spend on gorgeous designer gear. But that doesn't mean that you can't still look good.

Clothing crack-ups

**I'd love to wear cute miniskirts and stuff
but I've got short, fat legs.**

ARE YOU SURE your legs are *that* short and fat? Whatever, you probably can wear a mini as long as you follow a few simple rules:

★ Darker colours are more slimming than lighter ones.

★ Try wearing dark opaque tights that are at least fifty denier.

★ Really trendy shoes will take the emphasis away from your legs.

★ If you are going to wear a mini, make sure you are comfortable in it. If you keep pulling the hem down as if you are trying to cover up your thighs you will only bring attention to the fact that you aren't certain you should be wearing it and make others wonder whether you should.

★ When you think about the length of the skirt, bear in mind what's going to happen when you sit or bend down. Do you really want to show off your white-turned-grey knickers to the OAP on the other side of the bus?

Go and choose that mini now!

My mum reckons that I wear nothing but my jeans but I love my denim!

AS LONG as they aren't your really tatty pair, jeans can go with you virtually anywhere. In fact, because you'll be spending so much of your time wearing them, it's worth spending as much of your cash as you can on a decent pair that you will be truly happy with and feel stylish in. Here is the low-down on jean therapy:

★ Don't rush choosing the right pair of jeans. Be prepared to try at least half a dozen pairs before you select.

★ Buy jeans that have been cut for girls rather than boys. Boys tend to have narrower hips than girls so their jeans will look a bit tight around your bum.

★ Don't necessarily be tempted by the designer label. You are often paying for the label rather than the cut.

☆ Don't go for a pair that are covered in large but unknown labels as they will almost certainly look seriously naff.

☆ Beware of fake designer labels! You can usually tell if a pair is fake because they will have a 'cheaper' look about them: the rivets and the buttons will be lightweight and flimsy-looking; the denim itself will be thinner; the actual label will probably appear badly printed; the stitching will be 'thin' and dodgy. It's fine if you want to buy a pair of fakes or imitations if they are really cheap and you know they are only going to last a short length of time. It's not fine, though, if you are being ripped off. The most likely place to find fakes is a street market. And remember, girls with power aren't ripped off.

But how can I find a style that is mine?

SOME lucky people just seem to know what suits them without even trying. But the rest of us have to spend some time (and probably some money on mistakes) before we find our own individual style. Here are the Style Steps:

Step one: Go through the clothes that you've already got. Sort them into piles of

    a what you like;

    b what you don't really like;

    c what you haven't worn for yonks;

    d what doesn't fit (either too big or too small).

Pile **a** will give you a good idea of your personal style so take a look at the clothes and work out why it is that you like them. Is it because you like the colours? Because the clothes that you've got in pile **a** can be worn together to make a few different outfits? Do these clothes feel the most comfortable? Do people tell you how great you look in them?

The clothes in pile **b** are just as revealing! Why don't you like them? Because they make you look too fat or too thin? You hate the colours? The fabrics are too plain or too fancy? You don't feel comfortable in them? Your best mate told you they make you look like an anorak? Your gran bought them for you for Christmas? You don't . . . that's enough! OK, OK, you don't like them. So now you've worked out why you don't like them, make sure that you don't buy things in those colours, with those necklines, waistlines, turn-ups, fabrics, or whatever, again!

So *why* haven't you worn the clothes in pile **c** for yonks? Could it be that piles **b** and **c** are fairly interchangeable? In other words, you haven't worn the clothes for yonks because you don't actually like them? Or are your piles **b**, **c**, and **d** really just one big heap of clothes? Because you don't like what doesn't fit and so you don't wear those clothes very often?!

Step two: Don't despair! Most of us have wardrobes with piles **b**, **c**, and **d** in them!

Step three: Decide what you are going to do with the clothes that you don't really want and don't think you're ever going to like. Perhaps you could run a clothes swap-shop with your mates? After all, just because you don't like the colour of a jumper doesn't mean to say that it is yucky. (Remember that you bought it so you must have liked it once!) Or you could go along to a charity shop and donate your stuff to a good cause. Either way, do something about that heap of rags rather than leave it to the moths in your

21

wardrobe – leaving the clothes in a cupboard will just make you feel more depressed and guilty about them. (You may need to mention this to your parents first, if you think they might object . . .)

Step four: Remember that the style police reckon that you wear ten per cent of your clothes ninety per cent of the time. The other ninety per cent you barely wear at all!

Step five: Sit down with a pen and piece of paper and write down the colours that you like and that you know make you look and feel good. Then list all the items that you prefer to wear (long skirts or short skirts? trousers rather than skirts? that sort of thing) and the styles that you prefer (round necks or polo necks? bootlegs or drainpipes?). Now pin this list inside the door of your wardrobe and make sure that you look out for these types of clothes when you (or your mum) go shopping!

Step six: Be careful at the sales! Don't buy something just because it has been reduced by ninety-nine per cent. If the garment doesn't match up to your step five list, *don't buy it*!

Step seven: Look after the clothes in pile **a**. Hang or fold clothes properly before putting them back in a closet or chest of drawers. If the zip on your bootleg jeans breaks, fix it yourself or arrange for someone else to help you fix it. If a button has fallen off your favourite shirt, sew it back on a.s.a.p. And never put away clothes that are dirty! Sloppy, sloppy! When you go to wear your favourite clothes next time, do you really want your stale body odour to smell more than your body mist?

Step eight: Take someone with you when you go shopping and ask them what they really think of the clothes that you are thinking of buying. Whoever it is needs to be someone that you know will be honest! So don't take your boyfriend (who may only tell you what he thinks you want to hear) or your mum (who may only tell you what she approves of) and don't ask the shop assistant (who may only be interested in selling what she's got in her shop). If your best mate really is your best mate, take her because she'll probably be one of the only people in your life who is likely to tell you that your bum looks like the size of a bus in those Lycra cycle shorts!

Step nine: If you can't stop thinking about the underwear you are wearing because your knickers keep getting in a twist or your bra strap keeps on slipping down, you are wearing the wrong undies! And if you can see where the elastic on your knickers stops through your skirt or trousers . . . well, oh dear. Never wear knickers that are too small (all those bulges and VPLs – visible panty lines – just aren't attractive) or too big (you don't want your knickers to fall down at the bus stop, do you?). For advice on bras, see page 25.

The GIRL POWER Clothing Checklist

☆ If you feel good in it, you will look good too.
☆ Dress for yourself – not to attract boys.
☆ Never wear clothes that are dirty or that need fixing – you just won't feel good in them.
☆ Wear the right clothes for the right occasion.

☆ Wear the right size – not the size you wish you could slim down to or used to be.

☆ If you wear something very tight, short and sexy you may get unwanted attention. So be cool.

YOUR FIGURE

SOME of us are bigger and some of us are smaller than others. Either way, there are bits of your body that you can do something about (like perhaps your weight and any wobbly bits) but there are other bits that you are born with (like the size of your feet or the width of your hips). Girls with power have worked out how to make the most of what they've been given and make the world look up and say 'Yes!'

Anatomy anarchy

**My feet are so big they are embarrassing!
I keep tripping over my own feet and I can never find
shoes to suit me.**

IT'S A FACT that during the time of your life when you are still growing, your bones are getting longer. But the problem is that your bones don't really co-operate with each other and don't necessarily grow at the same time. It's fairly typical for most girls' feet to grow faster than the other bones in their bodies and most people's feet grow to their full length (perhaps as young as ten or eleven) way before they reach their final height.

Try not to be too self-conscious of your tootsies: scuffing your feet will only make people notice your toes – when they probably hadn't before that! Your shoes should be comfortable: if you walk around in shoes that are pinching you will only walk badly and draw attention to your feet again. If you think that people are staring at your feet, you might not want to wear shoes that are brightly coloured. Instead, stick to darker shoes that don't have fancy details like jazzy buckles or laces. However, if you think that people are staring at your toes, you might want to wear some more colourful or even outrageous shoes to give them something to look at! Do what makes you feel happiest.

If you find it difficult to find shoes in your size, look in your local telephone directory for shops like Long Tall Sally who stock more styles in larger sizes. Some of the high street shoe shops also have a range of larger shoes. And if you see someone when you are out and about who also has larger feet but great shoes, why not go up to them and say 'Where did you buy those great shoes?'. There's no need to mention the size of their feet – they'll just be flattered that you like their style!

My boobs are huge – I'm sure people stare at me when I run for the bus. My sister reckons her boobs are too small. How can we both learn to live with them?

BY getting a bra that fits! The bra manufacturers reckon that most women spend a large part of their life wearing bras that aren't the right size. So go along to a shop and get yourself fitted by a proper fitter. Most shops that sell underwear will have at least one assistant who knows how to do this properly – and discreetly. Don't be embarrassed! First of all, the person wielding the tape measure is going to be a woman and not some dead ringer for the Man. United forwards. Secondly, she's probably going to be a woman like your gran – so she's not likely to be unsympathetic to how nervous you might be feeling. Thirdly, the fitter is not going to start measuring you up in public – more likely there will be a special fitting-room where you can be fitted and where you can try on some bras to see if they fit. It's important to remember that once you know the size of bra you should be looking for, not all manufacturers' bras in that size will necessarily be a comfortable fit for you. If you find one brand that's just right it might be worth sticking with it.

If a bra fits properly it will keep a big bust under control and make a smaller one look like it exists. Big boobs can also be reduced by wearing a minimiser bra. Small boobs can be enhanced with a padded bra. If you do a lot of sport, wear a sports bra so that your bust (which has no muscle to keep it under control) won't jump up and down like live rabbits when you run for the ball.

Be proud of your bust, not ashamed of it. Breasts are a sign that you are developing into an adult with your own identity and personality. You may start to develop your bust as young as nine or not until you are sixteen – neither of these ages is wrong or right, they are just *you*.

It's not my top end that's the problem – it's my bum! I wear trousers that are at least one or two sizes bigger than the tops that I need. I probably take up two seats on the bus instead of one!

ISN'T life such a pain? Why should it be that the boys get the slim hips and the women get the curvy ones? Unfortunately, almost all girls' bodies have bits that are different sizes (if all your bits are the same dress size then congratulations – and get out of here!) and this has a lot to do with what we've inherited from our parents and grandparents. You see, if your mum has got a big bum, there is a good chance that you are going to have one too – sorry all mums out there! Now, if your bum is not just broad but wobbly as well, there is an obvious solution – to cut back on the calories and take up a bit of exercise. This will slim and tone and it is the toning which is probably the most important bit in making a better bottom! It simply doesn't matter to anyone else what size your butt is, but the fact is that if it isn't wobbling everywhere then you won't feel self-conscious about it, will you?

You can also make a difference to your appearance by choosing the right clothes which will slim down your hip department rather than drawing attention to it. So avoid overly-tight and also overly-baggy trousers. Make sure that the waist fits you rather than being so tight that it makes you look as if you have a ridge of flesh sitting on top of the waistband. Wear plain colours and don't allow any stripes or seriously fancy patterns to enter your wardrobe.

I'm fat and wobbly all over – I know that I've got to take care about what I eat but I just can't seem to stop noshing!

BEING big can be beautiful – just look at Dawn French for a start. But if being big makes you personally unhappy, then you ought to do something about it before it takes over your life and takes away all that girl power you've been mustering. Only a properly balanced diet, taken with the right amount of exercise, is going to make you lose weight the right way – which is slowly and permanently. Perhaps the best way to slim and trim is to first of all have a word with your mum and dad. They need to know what you are doing so that they can help you to achieve your goal. (There is also a chance that if they need to lose a few pounds then they can diet with you and share the pound-loss with you.) You should then take the advice of an expert about exactly what weight you should be aiming to reach – and this will depend on your height and your build. Now either your doctor or a registered and properly organised slimming club (such as Weight Watchers) will be able to advise you on this. Here are the girl power diet tips:

☆ Don't go anywhere near any lotions or potions that claim to make you lose weight. They don't work!

☆ Don't yo-yo diet. That means, don't keep going on a diet, lose weight and then binge on food and pile on the pounds again, then go on another diet, lose weight . . .

☆ Don't expect to lose a huge amount of weight straight away. If you are on a balanced diet then the weight-loss will be slow, controlled and, above all, permanent.

☆ Don't go on a diet just because someone else tells you to. Go on a diet because the end goal is what *you* want to achieve.

☆ Joining an organised diet club will mean that other people know what you are going through and will be able to sympathise on the bad days.

☆ Taking exercise burns up more of the calories than sitting on the sofa and flexing no muscles other than those in your fingers, working the remote control.

☆ Be realistic about the weight you should really be. If you set yourself an unrealistic goal it will be impossible to achieve and it will make you feel negative about yourself. And, as you know, girls with power feel positive!

I'm worried about a friend of mine. She's really pretty and she used to have a great figure. But a few months ago she started a diet and she's lost a lot of weight, although she still reckons she needs to lose some more. She's also become an exercise fanatic. Do you think I'm just feeling jealous because she's slimmer than me?

ALL OF US know someone whose figure is better than our own. But girls with power know that you do what you want about your own figure and leave it at that. If you are doubting that your mate looks as good as she used to, it doesn't sound like you're feeling jealous, does it? In fact, it sounds as if your friend has lost track of her girl power and is thinking that if she controls her weight to a complete extreme that somehow she can get back in control of her life. Someone once said a really stupid thing, which was that 'you can never be too rich or too thin' which, as any girl with power can work out very quickly, is a load of nonsense. If you are too thin, you don't have any energy or vitality and can make yourself seriously ill – so you certainly won't have any girl power. If you think one of your friends – or even you – has an eating disorder which makes them lose control of their dieting, they should be pointed in the direction of help immediately. You can get this from a doctor, the school nurse, or from a teen-help organisation (find out more about these in your local telephone directory). Don't try to tackle the problem on your own – tell parents or a teacher, someone who can help and share the pressure or knowledge.

The GIRL POWER Body Checklist

☆ Be proud of your figure and make the most of it.

☆ If, for whatever reason, you are worried about your figure, do something about it rather than just worrying about it.

☆ Wear the right size of underwear.

☆ Get your posture right and you will help any of the other problems that you think you might have.

☆ There's loads of life out there to enjoy – so don't waste any of it by spending your time just contemplating the possibility of your knees being too wobbly.

THE SHOPPING EXPERIENCE

SHOPPING should be fun but so often it turns out to be a frustrating event where you can't find what you want or the shop that you think is the one for you . . .

Shopping Basket Cases

I get really put off by the assistants in some shops – they make me feel as if I don't have the right to walk through the door!

IF the assistants are that awful you could try talking to them with your feet by simply walking out of their store and never entering its hallowed environment again. Or why not go into the shop with your mates – or even your mum – for courage? Even if you aren't seriously going to buy something from the store, you have as much right as anyone else to look at the goods – as the assistant well knows.

However, bear in mind that it might be that the shop has a policy about under-eighteens: some shops don't let you enter in groups, others don't let you in without someone over the age of eighteen. And don't be a twit and go into a clothes shop with a melting ice cream or a bar of chocolate in your hand – it will be dead embarrassing to be asked to leave because of that!

I've got a friend who manages to find really brilliant outfits at jumble sales and charity shops but all I've ever found has been a nasty nylon jumper. Any tips?

GO BACK and think about your Style Steps (page 20) and consult your list of things that you know suit you. Take the list with you to the jumble sale and only look at things that match up to your list. Remember that at jumble sales the items may not have been cleaned or pressed. If they haven't, try to imagine what they might look like when they've been smartened up. Beware of moth holes, rips in the fabric, missing buttons and broken zips. But remember that buttons and zips can often be replaced inexpensively. Jumble sales are also a great place to find cheap and cheerful jewellery, handbags, belts and scarves.

The other places to find second-hand clothes are charity shops, which are usually a step up from a jumble. Charity shops have usually cleaned up the garments on sale (which may well be reflected in the price you pay) so you will have a more instant idea of the suitability of the clothes. You may also have more opportunity of trying on the clothes in the privacy of a fitting-booth.

Again, you should look out for jewellery and accessories – in fact, Oxfam shops have a great line in ethnic jewellery which is worth looking out for. Make a habit of popping into your favourite charity shop now and then. Remember, you don't have to buy something every time you visit. It's the choosy girls who have power, because they only buy what's right for them.

Finally, remember that stylish clothes don't have to cost a fortune. It's the way you wear them that is important – and if you wear what you know suits you and what you feel good in, you will be wearing it well. Now that's girl power.

The GIRL POWER Guide to Shopping

☆ Shopping should be fun – if it isn't, go home and try again another day.

☆ If something you bought isn't right when you get it home, take it back to the shop as soon as possible.

☆ Always keep the receipt – you'll need it if the item disintegrates three months later.

☆ If you take something back, don't apologise to the assistant. Make it clear that this is their problem which they are going to sort for you.

☆ Don't buy on impulse, even in the sales.

☆ Walk into the shop with confidence and all your girl power mustered. That way the assistant will be happy to help.

YOUR HAIR

IF you are pleased with the way your hair looks, the chances are you will feel great about the rest of you. So it's a good idea to spend some time getting your hair the way you want it – but without being a slave to your locks!

Follicle Follies

My hair is so greasy I practically have to place kitchen paper round my shoulders to soak up the drips! Help!

WELL, you should obviously be using a shampoo for greasy hair for a start. Choose a good quality shampoo that doesn't strip your hair of its goodness as well as washing out the grease. Some people reckon that washing your hair every day actually makes it more greasy because it stirs up the sebaceous glands (the ones the grease comes from) in your scalp. But, quite frankly, if you feel better because your hair is clean each day, then go for it and wash it in the morning before you go out of the house.

Go easy on the mousses, gels and sprays though, if your hair is greasy. If you use them a lot they will build up in your hair and form a sort of coating on the outer layer of each strand of hair, making it look dull and lank. If you think you have got a build-up, try using one of the special shampoos you can buy which will take away the residue of all the products.

If your hair is really greasy you might want to consider having a perm done. The chemicals in the perming solution are quite harsh and tend to dry out the hair, which would certainly help the grease. But don't have a perm unless you are certain that it is what you want, and definitely don't even think about doing a perm yourself or letting your mates or your mum loose on it – unless she's a professional hairdresser, of course!

How do you find the right hairdresser?

YOU NEED to find a hairdresser who makes you feel good, rather than one who makes you feel like you've done something nasty in their chair. Hang around outside some of the hairdressing salons near to you on a Saturday morning (which will probably be their busiest day) and look at the girls coming out. Ask the ones who look great who cut their hair – they'll be flattered and pleased to tell you. Then find out how much the salon charges for a cut and blow-dry. (It may be that there is a scale of prices depending on the seniority of the hairdresser, so go for the one you think you can afford to pay for, if he or she is one whose cutting you've liked on other people.) Alternatively, if you know someone with a terrific hairstyle, why not ask them who does their hair? (And then ring up the salon to find out how much they charge before you get a nasty shock!)

When you ring up for an appointment, tell the receptionist that you want a 'cut and blow-dry', which basically means that you will have your hair washed, conditioned, cut and then blow-dried. If the salon operates a sliding scale of prices, tell them the level of the stylist that you are prepared to pay for (something like 'with a junior stylist, please') or if there is no scale of fees just tell them that you've not been there before. Some hairdressers advertise for house models which means that they are looking for girls who are prepared to have their hair done by trainee hairdressers or by experienced stylists who are trying out new methods. This can be a great way to have your hair cut very cheaply, or even for free. But there are some important factors for you to consider before you let anyone loose on your locks:

☆ Clarify that you will have the final say in what gets done to your hair. Don't let them dye or perm your hair if that isn't what you want. If you have long hair and don't want it chopped off, make that totally clear before the hairdresser starts brandishing those scissors – even at the time you make the arrangement.

☆ Find out how long they think it's going to take. House models are sometimes expected to hang around all night instead of the usual forty-five minutes.

☆ Is the house modelling likely to be a regular arrangement? If it is, and you are going to come back every six weeks or so, will they be doing a new look every time? (If they are, do you really think you can cope with a new look every couple of months?)

Finally, if you hate the idea of having a bloke run his fingers through your hair, make sure you ask for a female hairdresser when you book your appointment.

But how do I know what hairstyle is going to suit me?

HAVE a look through some magazines and cut out the photos of any styles and models that you like the look of. Take these along to the hairdressers with you and discuss them with the hairdresser. Ask their advice about what they think will suit you, bearing in mind the side that your parting naturally falls on, whether your hair is straight, curly or frizzy, thick or thin, if you want your hair shorter in style, or if you are actually growing it out from a shorter cut.

Don't feel nervous about saying what you think to the hairdresser. Remember that they will want you to come back because you have enjoyed having your hair done by them. And you won't do that, will you, if you haven't had a good time – and a good cut.

My hair looks great when I come out of the salon but how do I keep it looking good in between cuts?

DON'T FORGET to concentrate when the hairdresser is blow-drying your hair. Try to remember which part of your hair he or she dries first and what kind of brush they use to style it with. Ask them questions as they're styling your locks: why are they doing that? how can you do it at home? do they use mousse or gel before they start the drying and styling process? If you do the same things when you wash your hair at home, the chances are you will keep your hair looking good.

A decent haircut will usually last for about seven to eight weeks: at the end of that time, the hair will have grown so much that it will have lost its style. So, as a general rule, have your hair cut about every six weeks to keep it looking good – and you feeling girl-powered!

My hair is a sort of mousy-brown colour – it's so boring. Is there anything I can do about it?

SOME brown hair is neither light enough to be blonde nor dark enough to be a true brunette colour – and it can be referred to as mousy. But if your hair is in good condition and is shiny, well-cut and looked-after, it probably looks great whatever colour it is. However, if you still aren't happy with the colour, you could try one of the colour washes that are available in chemists. These are wash-in colours which will add colour that will last only a few shampoos. The idea is that the colour washes out gradually and the good thing is that they don't leave any root marks which advertise the fact that you've dyed your hair to the world! The problem with colour washes is that they are a bit messy to use. You will need to wear an old T-shirt and cover up your shoulders with an old towel that can catch any drips.

An instant way to brighten up your hair is to use one of the mascara-type colour products available. These put the colour only in the places you want it and the colours can be as crazy and varied as you want. The snag is that you will wash the colour out as soon as you next shampoo.

The problem with permanent hair colours is just that – they are permanent. The chemicals that are needed to radically change the colour of your hair are very strong, so permanent dyes are best left to professional hairdressers to apply. The only way to reverse most permanent hair dyes is to wait until all of the hair that has been dyed has grown out and been cut – which means that you will have to put up with the roots of your hair growing back and being a different colour to the ends. Not very pretty!

**I've got dreadful dandruff and leave flakes
of it all over my desk at school. How can I get
passionate with a boy if I'm going to leave
snow on his shoulders?**

FIRST OF ALL, are you sure it is dandruff? It could be psoriasis or an allergic reaction, so make an appointment to see your doctor and have the condition of your scalp checked out. If it can be treated medically (perhaps with a special lotion or shampoo) you might be able to sort out the problem, or at least get it under control, really quickly. If you have got dandruff, there are lots of excellent dandruff-control shampoos available from chemists.

The GIRL POWER Hair Checklist

☆ Never go out with dirty hair.

☆ If your hair looks great you will feel fantastic.

☆ Don't let a hairdresser talk you into something that you aren't sure about.

☆ Use good shampoos and hair products to keep your hair looking good.

☆ Have your hair regularly cut and styled.

☆ If a hairdresser is doing something that hurts or that you don't like, tell them!

☆ Have your hair cut in a style that suits your lifestyle as well as your face and body.

YOUR EYES

YOU see the world with your eyes so it's important to look after them. And looking after them is fairly simple: you need your eyes tested regularly and you need to make sure that you take all your make-up off properly every night *before* you go to bed.

Spectacle spotlights

**I've just been told I need to wear glasses.
How can I tell which specs are going to suit me?**

Here's how to spec select:

☆ Look through some magazines and cut out any photographs of celebrities who have swanky specs. You'll probably come across a few that you didn't even realise wore glasses. Remember that some stars who wear glasses don't actually *have* to wear them but *choose* to wear them so that they look cool. Take the photos with you to the optician's.

☆ Ask for advice and listen to it. The optician's will have lots of experience at choosing the right frames for faces. She or he can also advise you about the right glasses for your lifestyle – if you play sport, for instance.

☆ Don't hurry – the optician, or the optician's assistant is expecting you to take a long time. After all, these glasses are going to be a major part of your life for the next twelve months at least.

☆ Take advantage of any special offers the optician can offer. You might be able to buy one pair of glasses and get a second pair for free. Or you may be offered a pair of prescription sunglasses at reduced cost.

☆ Shop around. If you don't like the selection of glasses displayed at the optician's who has drawn up your prescription, you don't have to buy glasses from them. Take your prescription, along with your girl power, and visit another optician for your glasses. Better still, shop around *before* you book for your eye-test. Go into a number of opticians' and ask if you can browse through their stock of frames. If you explain what you are doing they should understand.

☆ Take along one of your mates or your mum so that they can offer their opinion too. If they are going to laugh out loud and say you look like a dingbat, they might as well do it before you buy the specs rather than once you've taken them home!

I look dead silly in my glasses – a right moron.
I hate wearing them!

WHO SAYS you look silly in them? Is it just you feeling self-conscious? Or is it someone else who has said you do – and if so, do you actually rate their opinion? Having said all that, if you really do hate wearing them, have you considered the alternative? Contact lenses come in four different types:

☆ Hard lenses are, well, hard! They are the longest-lasting contacts you can buy but it will also take you the longest time to get used to wearing them. Hard lenses are also the cheapest.

☆ Soft lenses are the easiest ones to get used to wearing but they won't last as long as hard lenses.

☆ Gas-permeable lenses are somewhere in between hard and soft contacts in price, the time it takes to get used to wearing them, and also the length of time they are likely to last.

☆ Disposable lenses are the easiest lenses to care for because you can either get ones that last a week before you throw them away or you can get ones you throw away after wearing them for only a day. But they are luxury lenses because they don't come cheaply!

Your optician will be able to advise you about the type of contact lenses that are best suited to your eyes and your lifestyle. She or he will give you important information about caring for and cleaning your lenses, which is vital if you want to be able to continue wearing your lenses always. It's no joke to say that not cleaning your lenses properly, or using the wrong cleaning solutions to do it can cause eye infections which can lead to permanent problems and not being able to wear your lenses ever again.

Remember that in very rare cases, some people can't wear lenses. But it's most likely that you will be able to wear lenses and, once you have collected them, you will be offered a number of follow-up appointments at which the optician will check that your lenses and eyes are compatible and healthy. It's important to keep these appointments, even if you think you don't have any problems with the lenses.

Then get your lenses checked every twelve months – perhaps at the same time that you have your annual eye-test. Remember that some types of contact lenses will only last for a year anyway.

The GIRL POWER Eye Checklist

☆ Always take your make-up off properly.

☆ Change your mascara about every eight weeks to stop the bugs inside the tube from growing.

☆ Have your eyes tested about once a year.

☆ If you wear contact lenses, don't think you can get away with skimping on keeping them clean – you can't.

☆ Don't rush choosing a new pair of specs – they are going to be a major part of your girl power look!

YOUR TEETH

MAKE the most of your teeth as they can make a big difference and you don't want to become self-conscious about your smile! There's a lot you can do yourself to make sure that your teeth are looking their best – so there are no excuses!

Brushing my teeth is so boring, though!

You might think so, but wouldn't life be even more boring if you
didn't have any teeth? You probably wouldn't look too great and
it might just be a bit difficult to munch on your food – so going
out for a hot dinner-date with your fave rave wouldn't be on very
often, would it? The tooth fairy says:

☆ Clean your teeth every morning, after breakfast, and every
night, just before you go to bed.

☆ Clean your gums and between your teeth with dental floss
or dental ribbon. There will be instructions about how to do
this on the packet but, for best advice, talk to your dentist or
the dental hygienist at the dental practice you go to. Cleaning
your gums is just as important as cleaning your teeth because
gum disease (sometimes called gingivitis) can wear away your
gums, change their colour, and make your gums bleed.
Eventually, if it is left untreated, gum disease can make your
teeth fall out.

☆ Change your toothbrush regularly – at least every three
months but, again, ask your dentist for advice.

☆ If you wear a brace, make sure that you follow your dentist's
advice on how to clean your teeth and the brace properly.

☆ Don't eat loads of sweet things and avoid sugary drinks
(including tea and coffee with sugar). Quite literally, sugar rots
the enamel on your teeth, so if you do eat sweet things, try to
brush your teeth soon afterwards.

☆ You can use a mouthwash to help you keep your teeth clean

and your breath fresh. Some are meant to be swilled around your teeth and gums before brushing so read the instructions on the label of the bottle to make sure you are using the mouthwash the correct way. However, don't think that you can use a mouthwash so that you don't need to bother brushing as well. *Brushing* your teeth is essential.

Sometimes I think my breath smells. How can I tell?

WELL, if you think it smells, then it probably does. Some people reckon that you can cup one of your hands and then exhale a deep breath into it. If you sniff the exhaled air straight away, you may get a whiff of what your breath smells like. It's up to you if you want to try this test!

Mouthwashes or even a mint will help you to keep your breath pleasant-smelling if you've got a temporary problem from drinking too much coffee or eating loads of garlic. But the only way to eradicate permanent bad breath (which is technically called halitosis) is to visit your dentist. You see, bad breath can be a sign that something is, or has gone wrong inside your mouth. Now that could either be your teeth or it could be your gums – either way, your dentist will be able to help you treat and get rid of the problem.

But I hate going to the dentist, what with all that poking and prodding and stuff.

WHY don't you like going to the dentist? If it's because you don't like your particular dentist, change to another dental practice (there's more info about how to cope with doctors and dentists in chapter six, Golden Oldies And Sophisticated Superiors). Or perhaps it's because you are worried about receiving treatment. If you are looking after your teeth as well as you possibly can, the dentist probably won't have to do anything to your teeth at your regular dental check-ups. But occasionally you may have to have a small cavity filled *which needn't be a terrifying experience* if you are in the hands of a good dentist.

Some twerps won't even go to the dentist when they are in pain from toothache. They endure days, weeks or even months of agony (and bad breath) just because they are too scared to visit a dentist. Pretty stupid, really, when you think that fifteen minutes in the dentist's chair will probably stop the pain almost immediately. Even more stupid when you think that the longer you leave the pain to throb the more damage is being done to the tooth, roots and gums and the longer the sit in the dentist's chair will be in the end!

My teeth are all crooked and wonky – some of them stick out as well. My mates call me goofy.

FRIENDS aren't always the kindest people, are they? Anyway, you really don't have to put up with crooked and wonky teeth, you know. Your dentist will be able to help you straighten out your teeth, sometimes with the help of a brace. Depending on the degree of the problem you have with the spacing of your teeth, you may be fitted with a brace that you only have to wear for a certain amount of time each day or night, or you may be fitted with a brace which you have to wear constantly for months or even a year or so. Your dentist (or perhaps you will be referred to an orthodontist) will give you regular check-ups to alter the brace according to the gradual correction that the brace is effecting on your teeth. He or she will also give you vital information about cleaning your teeth and your brace properly so that you can maintain a good standard of oral hygiene. Eventually the brace will be permanently removed to reveal stunning, straight, girl-powered toothypegs!

I wear a brace and it doesn't bother me most of the time. But whenever I speak, I seem to spit and spray people with saliva! It's so embarrassing that I sometimes don't even bother to join in with the conversation.

GO BACK to the specialist who fitted your brace and ask if they can give you advice about this. Everyone who has a brace fitted suffers this problem at first. If you think about it, you're not used to having anything other than your teeth and tongue (or food) in your mouth. So the idea of all the metal and rubber bands in your mouth is enough to make anyone dribble at first. Despite how you might feel now, you will get used to wearing your brace – so used to it that you will actually forget that you've got it on.

Whatever you do, don't withdraw and stop talking and making friends with people just because of your brace. That just ain't the girl power way. Remember, there are plenty of other people around who have braces too – and the more you talk with your brace on, the quicker you will get used to it and the quicker you will stop dribbling, spitting and lisping.

I've got used to wearing my brace now but I'm off to my cousin's wedding soon. How can I look my best with a brace on?

WHY NOT go in your best dress or trouser suit with matching braces on your teeth? You don't have to have just plain white rubber bands on your braces these days – your dentist should be able to fit different colours (just like you can get different colours of mouthguards for sport). So be daring, flash your multicoloured brace at people – and flash your girl power with it!

The GIRL Power Teeth Checklist

☆ Visit the dentist as regularly as he or she recommends.

☆ Brush twice a day or at least before you go to bed.

☆ If your teeth look good you'll feel brilliant.

☆ Don't be ashamed to have a brace – when it comes off you're going to have fantastically dreamy pearly whites.

☆ Don't put off sorting out any pains.

3

Confidence

OK, so we know that girl power is all about confidence. But how do you actually set about *becoming* confident? Here are some suggestions for building confidence, and keeping it!

LIKING YOURSELF

YOU may well look around you and think (at least, now and then) that other girls are funnier, brighter, more popular, even prettier than you are. And even though you know that there is a good chance they are feeling the same way, it doesn't make *you* feel any better. Girl power is all about believing in yourself. And you will only start to believe in yourself when you begin to like yourself. So take a closer look at what *you* have to offer. Then make the most of it and start oozing personality.

Yes, I'd love to be vivacious and witty and make everyone say 'Hey, wow!' about me but I'm just a plain person without heaps of interesting things to talk about.

47

LET'S just get it straight now: there isn't anyone in this world who has nothing to talk about! You do things, you have friends, you have relations, you have interests – so you automatically have things to discuss. The problem with being shy about coming forward is that it makes us think that we must be boring and that people won't be interested in us. This just isn't the case.

Girls with power know that they don't need to pretend to be anyone other than who they already are. You are yourself with your friends and they like you and enjoy being with you – so why shouldn't other people too? And when you are talking about things that really interest you and make you feel passionate about them, you will be talking animatedly and with total feeling for them – in other words, you will be vivacious.

A friend of mine is really funny and she's always making witty remarks about things. All the kids at school think she's fantastic and absolutely love her. How can I learn to drop jokes into the conversation like she does?

PEOPLE who can make jokes at the drop of a hat are incredibly lucky – and very rare! There are very few people who can do it successfully so don't feel like you've done something wrong if you can't. In fact, the harder you try to be funny, the more impossible it will probably be. So try to relax about being witty and just say what you think, when you think it, and if you want to. You'll probably find that you are quite capable of making jokes when you just aren't trying! Girls with power accept that the hardest time to try to be funny is when you are feeling under pressure. Anyway, life is made up of all different kinds of people. Imagine how boring it would be if everyone went around being witty and dynamic and, perhaps, a little overpowering. It would be exhausting for a start, and boring – even irritating – for most of the time.

I'm just not a very chatty person, though. I prefer listening to my mates most of the time – so won't new people I meet think I'm a bit dull?

THEY are no more likely to think *you* are dull than you are to think that *they* are. *Do* remember that you are *you* and people should like you for that. If they don't, they don't – and you should never try to be someone else for the sake of trying to please someone else! Got that?

Anyway, one of the reasons why all your current mates like you is probably *because* you are such a good listener. Good listeners are important in life: you can tell them your problems and they will be prepared to listen patiently; you can tell them your hopes; you can confide your secrets to them. And the other brilliant thing about good listeners is that they are often really good at giving advice in a controlled and reasonable manner, and they don't go round spouting off their opinions in an arrogant way. In fact, your mates must be especially happy to have a good listener like you around them.

Lots of people say I'm quite a bubbly sort of person. Some kids really seem to like me but others keep well away and kind of groan when they see me in the corridors at school. What am I doing wrong?

IT'S UNLIKELY that you are doing something wrong but it does sound as if you have got quite a powerful personality and that perhaps you use it all the time. There is nothing wrong with that but you might want to think about toning down some of your personality some of the time. The thing is that some situations require a quieter approach to them. Life is about experiencing all sorts of different situations and working out which is the best way to behave for each one and unfortunately there isn't really a better way of learning about it than actually doing it. But don't think that you are likely to bulldoze your way through situations and make a total, utter twit of yourself. Very few people are thick-skinned or stupid enough to get things completely wrong. At worst they may start a conversation in a loud and over-the-top way, but they will soon realise that the person they are speaking to is turned off by that and will start to back off and quieten down a bit.

The fact that some people like you and other people don't is perfectly normal so don't waste your precious time worrying about it. Nobody can expect the whole world to be in love with them and they would be ridiculously hard on themselves if they thought that should be the case and therefore felt a failure. *You* like some people and don't much like others (you may even really loathe some people) so you shouldn't really be surprised to discover that other people feel the same about you. The world is full of all sorts of different people – that is what makes it so much fun!

The GIRL POWER Guide to your Personality

☆ Make the most of what you have already got rather than trying to change yourself into someone else.

☆ Being witty isn't the only way to be a success with people.

☆ Being a good listener is an art that not all of us have.

☆ Different types of people make life interesting.

☆ It's not your fault if not everyone likes you – no one is liked by everyone.

☆ You don't have to like everyone else.

☆ Be realistic about your best assets.

ROLE MODELS

YOU were born with a personality, but also with the ability to develop your personality. It's entirely up to you to work out what you want to do with it. Finding a role model can help to build up your confidence: when you enter a situation that makes you nervous, you can think about what your chosen role model would do in those circumstances, try to act likewise and get your courage from them!

But what exactly is a role model?

YOU may already have a role model but not yet have realised it! Is there a female pop star or an actress that you think is really fantastic? Or perhaps you admire one of your older girl cousins or an aunt? If you do, then you've got your role model.

Now think about what it is that you like about this person: is it their looks, their clothes, the things they talk about, the way they ooze confidence? Whichever of these things it is (and it could be more than one, or all of them), see how you can apply the way they do it to your own life.

**My mate spends all her time copying a girl in
the sixth form. I'm worried that she's beginning to
get obsessed with her.**

OH DEAR. This can be the downside of role models, if girls let the situation get out of hand. If a girl is in control, she will realise that she needs to *adapt* the things she likes about her role model to suit her rather than to make herself a clone of someone else. And if the role model is a person they know, any initial flattery of knowing that someone admires them will soon wear a little thin when they can't wear a pair of boots for two seconds before their admirer has got an identical pair.

A role model should provide inspiration, not the mould for a clone.

The GIRL POWER Guide for Having a Role Model

☆ You don't have to do everything that your role model does.
☆ You can have a role model that you know personally or just observe from afar.
☆ Adapt the role model's best things to suit your own life rather than the other way round.

NERVOUSNESS, BLUSHING AND SWEATING: THE GIRL POWER APPROACH

SOME people suffer from all of these things. Others only have one of the problems – but there are ways to deal with them.

**It's awful. Every time there is a boy or a man around
I start to sweat. My armpits are like floodgates opening!**

ONE of the worst things about moving up from childhood to being a teen is that you start to sweat. Most people only perspire when they are doing sport or exerting a lot of physical energy on something. But others aren't so lucky and the sweat starts to flow when they are feeling nervous or anxious about something. Fortunately the wonders of modern science have helped most of us by producing some great antiperspirants which come with a deodorant as part of them. These stop most of the sweating – and help stop us from smelling when the sweat that does escape dries. Having a bath or shower every day can also help us to keep the odours away.

Remember that:

☆ Everyone sweats – it's normal!

☆ If you feel self-conscious of perspiring (that's the posh word for it!), always remember to wear deodorant and try to wear tops which aren't tight under your arms and which don't show sweat marks easily. Keeping your armpits hair-free will also help to keep the pong at bay!

However, if you think that you sweat an incredible amount more than your underarm magic can cope with, go along to see your doctor. Some people (and remember that this is very rare) suffer from a medical condition which affects the way in which their sweat glands work and there is a small possibility that you may be one of them. Either way, your doctor will be able to put your mind at rest (also remember that the problem is always much more acute to the person who is suffering than to anyone else and it's likely that no one else will notice) or give you some treatment which will help you.

Some people sweat across their brow or in the palms of their hands. Obviously, you can't run a roll-on along these areas! What you can do, though, is carry a hanky with you and wipe your forehead with this, or you could discreetly wipe your hands on your skirt or trousers (and try not to clench your hands or tense them). And if you are really worried about it all seeming so obvious, why not say something like, 'Gosh, it's very hot in here, isn't it?'. That way you are acknowledging the situation rather than trying to ignore it and possibly sweating even more!

I blush every time I start a conversation with someone I don't know – whatever sex they are.

BLUSHING can be embarrassing and regrettably there isn't much you can do about covering the blushes up. But remember that:

☆ You are not the only one it happens to so lots of people will understand how you feel.

☆ As quickly as the blush arrives it will go away.

☆ You can always say, 'Wow, it's hot around here.'

☆ If your blushing always happens in the same types of situations, you can do your best to avoid those situations or at least make them less stressful. When you feel the blush coming on, try taking your mind off it by reciting a nursery rhyme or limerick in your head. It might help to hold the blush back a bit.

I get so nervous that I can't speak!

NERVOUSNESS can affect people in all sorts of ways: some people stutter, some people can't stop talking, others can't speak at all, and some people start to shake or twitch. Whichever way your nervousness affects you, try the following:

☆ Count to twenty – or, better still, count from twenty backwards. That will take your mind off the situation that is making you nervous.

☆ If you are with other people and are waiting for a test or something, try diffusing the tension by saying, 'Boy, am I nervous!' You'll probably find that everyone else is too and that by sharing your nerves around you are all helping each other!

☆ Say nothing if you think that your nerves will make you say something you will regret.

☆ Go for a short walk rather than stand around shaking.

I hate it when the conversation dries up! I just don't know what to say.

FIRST OF ALL, if the conversation has dried up, everyone else is in the same situation as you! This classic 'three-minute silence' situation happens to all sorts of people frequently. Remember that everyone will feel just like you and is desperately trying to be the one who breaks the silence. If your confidence is a bit shaky, try *thinking* about what you want to say *before* you open your mouth and say something you instantly regret.

If you are feeling a bit more in control, try saying:

☆ 'Was it something I said!' (Say it sarcastically and dramatically to try to make a joke of it, if you think you can carry it off.)

☆ 'Heavens. I think an insect just landed in my meal!'

(Obviously this one only works if you are eating!)

☆ 'Isn't that so-and-so over there?' (Only works if you are in a public place or standing next to a window.)

If you don't feel that you can say something as positive as that, just say something like, 'Hey, none of us are very good at this, are we?' Whatever happens, the silence will probably seem far longer than it actually is.

The GIRL POWER Strategies for Coping with Difficult Situations

☆ Remember that they happen to everyone else too!

☆ If you're in a situation and someone says something clever (but simple) to get the conversation going, try to remember it for future use.

☆ If you really can't handle the stress, say 'Excuse me' and walk away (perhaps to the loo) for a minute and then come back when you are feeling more in control.

☆ Don't be shy of having your own opinions and expressing them in public. People are always interested to hear what others think and have to say.

☆ Don't be crushed by someone if they don't agree with you. They are entitled to their opinions too!

BLOKES WHO ARE TOO CLEVER FOR YOUR OWN GOOD

THERE is nothing worse than a loud-mouthed boy who thinks he is a gift to the female world, is there?

I hate it when some boy criticises me or one of my mates! They always do it in public and put down the girls with their unkind comments.

WELL, you see, they think they have got boy power but in fact they have just got an over-inflated idea of how clever, funny and important they are. And boys are usually far worse when they are in a group than when they are on their own. Next time a boy behaves in some macho way, try using one of the following:

Three GIRL POWER Strategies for Coping with Clever Dicks

☆ When they come out with some sarcastic and sexist or unpleasant comment, don't get angry – get even. Say, 'Well you should know, of course, look at all the girls that *aren't* standing anywhere near you.'

☆ When they do something gross like touch up some girl when she is walking past, try screaming, at the top of your voice, 'Get your hand off my boobs/bum/whatever!' That should have them diving for cover – but you have to be really angry to do it, although you almost certainly will be if that happens to you. Then report them to a teacher because they have absolutely no right to behave that way.

☆ Just look at them pityingly and say, 'You're just not worth the comment, are you? When you grow up, we might start talking to you. But we are not convinced.' Then continue your previous conversation or all of you walk away.

4

Your Friends

LIFE just isn't the same without friends: there's no one to have a laugh with when you realise what you look like with suction-fit Lycra bootlegs on; there's no one to cry with when you've just got the results of your exams; there's no one to share a magazine with; there's no one to be a couch potato with when your face has broken out in zits on Saturday night. In fact, a good friend could well be worth more than their weight in gold because they will be:

☆ honest;

☆ good fun;

☆ there when you need them;

☆ someone you can argue with but still be a friend afterwards;

☆ able to laugh with you rather than at you and

☆ willing to share your friendship with others.

THINK ABOUT IT. Do you match up to being a good friend yourself? Because if you don't, how can you expect your mates to stick around? A girl with power has lots of girls to be powerful with!

SOME people live in the same area for ever so they know loads of people at school and also in the neighbourhood. Other people move house and school because of their parents' jobs. Either way, we aren't born with a set of friends that will never ever change and there are always days when we meet new people. Try to use these occasions as a chance to make new friends.

Friendly feelings

I've just moved to a new town and I'm going to start at a new school after the holidays. I was at my last place for years – all my mates moved from primary school with me, they've just always been my mates. And now I'm on my own in a place I don't know. Everyone's bound to have mates of their own already.

WELL, just like you, the kids at your new school will probably have changed school with friends they made at primary school. But there will also have been kids who joined from other schools that they didn't know, and they'll have had to make friends too. It's rotten to find yourself on your own as the new kid on the block – except when you think of all the opportunities it gives you! Try to think of it as something exciting rather than terrifying. Be yourself. And remember, most people are probably really pleased to have a new person in the class – it's always interesting! So make the most of it and add some new friends to the ones you've already got.

The GIRL POWER Friends Checklist

☆ On your first day at your new school you'll have the chance to make about thirty new chums straight away! There will probably be that many kids in your class and, OK, so not all of them will be your sort of people but there's a really good chance that at least one or a couple of them will.

☆ Ask the kids in your class about any local youth clubs or school clubs that exist in your area.

☆ If you spot someone at the same bus stop as you in your new school's uniform, start up a conversation with them. Even if you feel shy, you could always ask a simple question like, 'Excuse me, do you know when the next bus is?' If they are dead shy, or maybe even dead boring, they might just reply, 'In ten minutes' – but it could be the start of a much longer chat and perhaps even a friendship with someone who lives near you.

☆ Have a word with your teacher about any sports clubs and teams there are at your new school. By joining a team or just going along to improve your sports skills, you'll widen the number of people that you get the chance to meet and not necessarily just restrict yourself to the kids in your class.

☆ Don't restrict yourself to sports clubs either. Find out about other clubs or school societies (such as music, art, drama, debating or environmental groups) and exercise your girl power by discovering something new and exciting. You don't necessarily have to be brilliant at something to be in a group. Girls with power do things because they enjoy them – not necessarily because they excel at them.

SOME people can talk until the cows come home but other people find all that talk just makes their lips glue together. Either way, talking gets friendships going, so even if you find it difficult, keep trying to get the girl power gift of the gab!

Talk terrors

I've found out about these places to go to, but I haven't a clue what to say to anyone when I get there.

NEARLY everyone has butterflies in their tummy when they walk into a room full of strangers – so don't think you are on your own with this one! If you are scared at the thought of walking into a full room, think of someone you've seen who looked cool and confident (perhaps a movie star) entering a room. Chances are that they were terrified, but people can't see that. If you pretend to be confident and make your body language seem positive (see posture checklist, page 18), people will believe it – and you might start believing it too!

You will probably have made some sort of enquiry (say a phone call) to find out about the club or place you have come to visit for the first time. So, when you first arrive, why not start by saying to someone, 'Hello, I'm looking for Elizabeth. Can you tell me where she is?' Elizabeth (or Fred or Mrs Snodgrass, whatever his or her name is) will then be found and introduced to you. And then she, in turn, will almost certainly introduce you to some other people. Then you can start chatting about sport, singing, dance, or whatever your shared passion is that brought you to the club in the first place! If you've got nothing else in common, why not have some standard questions ready to ask, like, 'Have you lived round here for long?', 'Is it always this busy?' or 'Do you belong to any other clubs?' Open-ended questions, which need more than a yes or no answer, are also a really good way of starting conversation.

My problem is that I just can't stop talking!
When I'm nervous I just rabbit on and on . . .
People must think I'm really pushy.

FIRST OF ALL, you probably don't talk as much as you think you do – it's just that you are conscious of it, so you think about it more. If you find yourself rambling on, stop for a minute and say to the person you are talking to, 'What do *you* think?' or 'Do you agree?' or some other question. Then they will get a chance to talk – and you'll get the chance to get your breath back! Another thing to remember is not to interrupt people when they are talking because that is the time when people can start thinking that you are being pushy.

If you do have a tendency to gibber, just make a conscious effort not to jabber on about yourself too much. Tell people about the things you may have done before but don't drone on about how brilliant you are – that's guaranteed to turn folk off you. Try to ask people questions about themselves as well as telling them a little about what you've done.

Don't be tempted to exaggerate in order to try to impress. There is a good chance that the person you are talking to will realise, sooner or later, that you have been flexible with the truth which could make them wonder about everything else that you've told them. They will also get very tired of all your boasting. So be honest – and just be yourself! Girls with power don't need to pretend to be bigger or better because they like and appreciate who they are!

The GIRL POWER Chatting Checklist

☆ Remember that you are good enough for someone to want to make friends with.

☆ If you believe in yourself, other people will believe in you too.

☆ Don't lie about yourself to impress people – they are interested in you not someone you could be.

☆ You don't have to be the life and soul – just join in and people will appreciate it if you share in the fun.

KEEPING FRIENDS

IT'S a funny thing, but lots of people say that they know almost straight away when they've met someone that they really like and want to see more of – and not always 'someone' of the opposite sex! (If you want to find out more about meeting boys, see chapter five, Boys.) Some people call good friends 'soul mates' because they reckon that they understand *how* they are thinking or even *what* they are thinking about without even saying a word sometimes. But even if you have 'clicked' with someone and made friends with them, you've still got to make an effort to keep your friendship going.

Fostering friendships

**I met a really fun girl at netball practice last week
and she seemed to quite like me. I'd like to see more of
her other than at practice – what should I do?**

WHY NOT have a word with her at the next netball session and ask
her if she'd like to see a film, or perhaps come and help you choose
a new pair of trainers, and then go for lunch afterwards? You never
know, she might be planning to ask you the same thing herself!

**Surely being a good friend just
comes naturally, doesn't it?**

TO a large extent it should do. But here are some things that are
worth bearing in mind in order to keep your friendships sweet:

☆ Remember birthdays or any other special days in order to
show that you care.

☆ Be sympathetic if she's had a bad day (and then she should
be for you when it's your turn).

☆ Don't be rude about her boyfriends.

☆ Try not to be rude *to* her boyfriends.

☆ Do be honest and truthful about her boyfriends.

☆ Don't pinch her boyfriends.

☆ If you've made a new friend, try to share the friend rather
than keep them secret or to yourself.

☆ Don't keep secrets from her.

☆ If you've got a new boyfriend, tell her.

☆ Give your friend time as well as your boyfriend. There's
more about this in chapter five, Boys.

☆ If she asks you what she looks like in an outfit, tell her the truth. And if you have to tell her she doesn't look good, be as tactful as possible – perhaps break the bad news to her by comparing her looks to some disastrous outfit you once tried on in her presence!

I'm in the middle of doing revision for my exams and my best mate reckons that I'm ignoring her. My exam results are important to me – but so is my friend! What should I do?

EVERYONE needs time off now and then, even when there are exams on the horizon. The trick with life and friends is to keep them well-balanced – and one of the best ways to do this is to keep your best mate involved with what you are doing. Before you lock yourself in your bedroom for three weeks of non-stop cramming, try telling your friend that you are going to be revising over the next few weeks but can you pool your revision timetables and try to find at least one occasion each week when you can go out and have some fun? There's a good chance that your friend will also be revising for exams, so she should under-stand your problem. Of course, if you can trust yourselves to be serious and studious, perhaps the pair of you can do some of your revision together, particularly if you are doing the same subjects. That way you can join girl power forces. But remember that some people need to work harder than others or perhaps do so because they want to. Either way, a good friend will accept it if a chum wants to spend more time studying than her.

Ultimately, the thing to be is honest. Tell your mate that she's important to you but that your exams are too. Explain to her what is going on and that it is only for a few weeks and she should understand. If she doesn't and throws a wobbly, then you might start wondering if your friend really is the good mate that you thought she was. After all, a good friend should want to help you to do well, shouldn't she?

The GIRL POWER Keeping Friendly Checklist

☆ Remember a friendship takes two to make it work.

☆ Good friends won't get jealous if their best friend does something on their own or with someone else.

☆ Honesty always helps (but isn't an excuse to be rude . . .).

☆ Be the kind of friend to her that you want her to be to you.

☆ Never, ever, let boys get in the way of your friendship.

FIGHTING FRIENDS

IF you and your mates never fall out then you are lucky – and possibly either saints or just unique! All of life is about ups and downs so your friendships will be too. Which means that there will inevitably be days when you and your chums have disagreements, fights, arguments or whatever it is that you want to call falling out!

Combat questions

I've known my best mate for years – ever since primary school. Now she's gone and got herself a boyfriend and doesn't have time for me any more. I told her it was either him or me . . . and it seems like she's chosen him.

IT HURTS, doesn't it, when your mate suddenly finds a boy whose company she seems to enjoy as much as yours? But, be honest, could it be that you are feeling a bit put out because she got a boyfriend before you did? Of course, it may be that you don't even want a boyfriend but she obviously does want one. And you can't take her away from him. But you can still be her friend and see her some of the time, can't you? She's inevitably going to want to spend time with him so you will see less of her. But wasn't it a bit hasty to turn round and tell her it was you or him? Try and arrange to meet up with her on her own. Tell her that you are sorry about what you said and you still want to hang around with her some of the time. If she's a good mate, she'll value your friend-ship and will want to spend time with you. Just don't expect her to spend more time with you than with him.

The GIRL POWER Guide to Saying Sorry

☆ Don't sit back in a pigheaded way, waiting for your friend to come running to you. If you were the one who stepped out of line, it should be you that goes to your friend to make amends.

☆ Say sorry as quickly as possible after you've fallen out. The longer you leave an apology, the more resentment breeds and the harder it is to say.

☆ Backing down or saying you are sorry when you were wrong is not a sign of weakness. Far from it, it is actually a sign of being in control – it takes guts to admit that you were wrong.

☆ Choose a good time to speak to her – don't try to say sorry when she's with someone else, especially not her boyfriend.

☆ Try phoning her to make the first move and perhaps suggest that you get together to talk the thing over properly.

☆ Be honest and admit that you acted hastily.

☆ Say how much you value your friendship and that you don't want to lose it.

☆ Explain that you understand how she feels about her boyfriend and that you still think you two can remain friends.

☆ If she can't, or won't make friends again, do whatever you can to keep your cool. Don't say horrid things to her that you might regret later, and do your best to part in a civilised fashion. There's nothing worse than having to look the other way in embarrassment every time you see her at school or in a shop.

I've fallen out with my friend over something really silly – she bought a pair of boots exactly the same as the pair that she knew I was saving up for. It's her fault but I still want to be mates and she hasn't said she's sorry. What should I do?

IF you really value her friendship, however irritating it is that she got the boots before you did, why not make the first move and go and talk to her. It might be that she's feeling too embarrassed and guilty to come to you – and if she really is your friend and you are really hers, surely it doesn't actually matter who makes the first gesture towards making up? What really matters is that you are friends. And anyway, perhaps you should feel flattered that she likes your taste so much that she went out and bought those boots.

If, however, she repeatedly does things that upset you and doesn't make an effort to apologise, then maybe you should stand back and let her try to salvage the friendship if she really cares.

The GIRL POWER Fighting Checklist

☆ If you can sense tension and a possible fight, check out of the situation. Say something like, 'Hey, let's call it a day for now,' and head off for home rather than a confrontation. Try to talk about problems in a calm way to achieve a resolution rather than just to release anger.

☆ Don't be tempted to put words into her mouth and let yourself begin to think she said things she didn't.

☆ Make up sooner rather than later.

☆ Remember that no friendship is all ups with no downs.

☆ A good friend is not worth losing because of pride.

BULLYING

A recent survey says that seven out of every ten people has had some experience of bullying in their lives – and that includes adults and kids.

Bully bothers

It's not me and my friend who have fallen out,
it's her and another girl who keep having bust-ups.
In fact, this other girl has got it in for my friend and
she keeps picking on her. The other day, my friend said
she'd been told by the girl that if she didn't give her some
money then she'd rip up her topics folder. I'm worried
about it because my mate always used to be a good
laugh but now she seems really tense and quiet.

She doesn't even like to stay out much after school any more. She had a bruise on her face a couple of weeks ago and she told me that she'd fallen over but I'm beginning to wonder if she was actually punched by this girl. I suppose that what I'm trying to say is that I think my friend might be being bullied.

YOUR friend is very lucky to have a friend like you who is concerned about her – especially if you are going to help her get out of this difficult situation. First of all, have a word with your friend and ask her outright if this girl is picking on her and bullying her. If it makes it easier, say that you think this is what is happening and you want to be certain that it is so that you help her to sort the problem. If your friend tells you that it is true, remind her that it isn't her who is being weak. In fact, it is the girl who is doing the bullying that is weak (although she may not seem that way to your friend at the moment) which is why she needs to find someone like your friend to victimise – because doing so makes her feel like she's tough and strong.

Now that you've got this far, don't waste any time. You could tell your parents about what is happening to your friend if you think they can help you or give advice but, whatever you do, you should *immediately* tell your form tutor or your year head or even your head teacher. This bully needs stopping and she needs stopping fast. Whichever teacher you go to will want to interview your friend about exactly what has been happening and how often it has been happening. They will then take steps to deal with the girl concerned.

Don't be surprised if this bully girl turns out to be bullying other kids or has done in the past. And don't be frightened that she will take things out on you as well if you step in to help your friend. That's unlikely to be the case, as long as you tell someone in authority at your school and don't try any vigilante tactics on your own – which would just make things much worse. As soon as this bully is tackled by a teacher they are likely to back off. If they don't, then the teacher you originally reported it to should be told straight away and she or he will deal with the matter – if, of course, she or he hasn't been monitoring the situation all the time, which is more likely. This bully girl will be at risk of being suspended or expelled from the school if she continues. The important thing is always to tell an adult. If your friend denies there is a problem then you have to tread carefully – if you bulldoze your way into trying to sort things you could make her withdraw and stop confiding in you. But if you are convinced that there is a problem, do confide your fears to a teacher – they may be able to help, and you shouldn't have to carry the pressure of worrying about your friend by yourself. Your teacher will be able to speak to your friend (and can pretend that he or she has spotted that something's wrong) and can start helping her straight away. Remember, girl power isn't about being a hero, it's about using practical ways to help.

But my mate is being bullied by someone from another school. What can we do about that?

AGAIN, you and your friend shouldn't suffer in silence. Tell your parents and tell your teacher because there is a good chance that you will know which school this bully goes to. Then your teacher can have a word with the appropriate teacher at the bully's school and steps will be taken to put the whole horrid business to a stop. If you don't know which school it is and the bullying is getting nasty (or if the bully is part of a gang), have a word with your parents about reporting the matter to the police urgently. The police hate bullies just as much as everyone else and they may well be prepared to have a word with this bully and their parents to put a stop to it.

I just can't stand my stepbrother.
He's younger than me – my dad's new wife had him
just after my mum and dad divorced. Now every time I go
round to my dad's this little pest gets in my way and he
makes me so angry! He leaves his toys all over my stuff
and is always trying to poke around in my bag. Last week I
lashed out at him and thumped him behind the ear. I
didn't feel great at first but it did stop him. I told
him not to tell my dad though. Now I've got
him under control, haven't I?

BUT have you got yourself under control? It doesn't sound like it because it sounds as if you have turned into a bit of a bully. Think about it, this boy doesn't know any better because he is obviously much younger than you. He is clearly really happy to have you, his big sister around to see him and wants to make the most of his time with you. And it sounds as if you are a tincey wincey bit jealous of your dad giving him some of the time that you wish he spent with you. So, instead of being a girl with power and making the most of your time at your dad's, you have shown the weakness that all bullies have – which is to use brute force and strength over someone who is physically weaker than them rather than using their brains and any wisdom. A girl with power knows when to hold back and how to control her temper.

Try talking to your dad about the problem. Explain that you need space and privacy and ask if he can help come to an arrangement over this. Tell him that you need time alone with him – just like your stepbrother gets when you are not there. If you explain how you feel, rather than bottling all your feelings up, your dad should be sympathetic and you should begin to get the situation, and yourself, back under control.

The GIRL POWER Bullies Checklist

☆ However hard it is to deal with the problem, you have to sort it – whether you are the victim, a friend, or the bully.

☆ Deal with the problem soonest.

☆ Remember it is bullies who are the weak ones *not* their victims.

5

Boys

THE funny thing about boys is that, when you are younger, it's OK with everyone for girls to have friends who just happen to be boys. Then, suddenly, without warning, it becomes awkward to have them. *Why?* That's the big question – and it's probably got a lot of different answers. One reason is because boys don't seem to mature as quickly as girls: when you are entering your teens, they are often still worrying about conkers and chewing-gum. Another reason is that, at the same time, you might be starting to have periods, so you may prefer the company of girls who understand what you're going through (because they are going through the same things) rather than boys who won't understand and just make stupid jokes about it. Then, of course, you might have recently changed to an all-girl school and, sometimes, being in the company of girls most of the time somehow gets you out of practice of being with boys. Another thing that can happen is that, if you come across a group of boys together, they can start acting like morons instead of human beings – and who wants to spend time with a moron who they don't *have* to spend time with?

BOYS AS FRIENDS

THE THING about having girl power is that you know that life is all about having fun. What you need is friends, not necessarily a boyfriend.

Boy blushes

The boy next door is the same age as me and we used to go to primary school together and hang around together during the holiday. But since we've changed to single-sex schools we don't see each other so often and when we do, he gets all embarrassed and keeps saying things like 'I'm not your boyfriend, you know'. I know he's not – so why does he keep saying it?

HE'S probably made a whole new bunch of friends (who are bound to be boys) since he changed school – a bit like you made another load of friends as well. So, for a start, you don't need each other as friends as much as you used to, so don't worry if you don't see so much of each other. Also, his new mates have probably teased him about living next door to you because some stupid boys think that if you've got a friend of the opposite sex then she must be your girlfriend. So he could have got himself confused into thinking that *you* think that way as well and he might be worried that you fancy him (OK, OK, so that may be the funniest thing you've heard all year but if he doesn't think he's good-looking, who else – apart from his mum – is going to think that he is?).

Your BND (boy next door), like other boys of your age, may

not have grown up as quickly as you so it could also be that he just isn't interested in the same things as you at the moment. This may change over the next couple of years – but don't wait for it to happen as it just might not. So give yourself a break from hanging around with him as much as you used to. But don't stop talking to him completely because there is a good chance that if you got on well with him once, you will do again in the near future.

A friend of mine (a boy) came home with me after school to work on a project in my room. My mum went ballistic the other day when she heard. What's her problem?

IT might be that she's still carrying the excess baggage that your gran gave her when she was your age: that your mum would never ever have been allowed to have a bloke in her room unless she was related to them. Once she realises that your friend was there just to work on your project she'll probably be dead embarrassed that she ever mentioned it in the first place. The thing is, it's you that has to show your mum (and perhaps your dad, for that matter) that this boy is your friend – and that's all. Establish some rules: say that you'll always keep the door open when you're working, that he'll always be gone by nine p.m., that the same rules apply when you go round to his place. Remind your mum that you are, after all, the girl she brought up – so surely she'll trust you, won't she? Now that's being in control!

I get really embarrassed when my older brother has his mates round. If any of them speak to me I just go all pink and can't think of anything sensible to say.

LOTS of girls (and boys, for that matter) feel embarrassed and shy in front of older kids. For some reason, they seem so sophisticated and glamorous (OK, so we know that your older brother could hardly be glamorous, but other people's brothers could be) and you might think that you look unsophisticated and boring in comparison. Well, that's almost certainly not true about any girl with girl power! If you are feeling confident about yourself and your looks, you will feel more in control of the situation (take another look at chapter two, Your Image to check that you've got that sorted). But, if you feel a panic situation coming on when you walk into a room with boys, follow these steps:

☆ Stop! Now take a deep breath and exhale slowly.

☆ Walk into the room with a smile on your face (a natural one, not a manic-looking grin) and say 'Hi!'.

☆ If your mouth dries up, bite your tongue (not too hard)! This should make your saliva glands get to work to moisten your mouth again.

☆ If you can feel yourself going red, take a few more deep breaths to calm yourself down.

☆ If you find yourself feeling tongue-tied after someone speaks to you, try saying, 'Sorry, I didn't quite catch that, can you say it again?' and while you are listening to them repeating it, work out your answer.

☆ Don't worry about being supercool, funny or impressive. They probably won't be – so just be friendly.

If you carry on finding it difficult to talk with your brother's friends, perhaps you should just avoid them for a short while and wait until you get your confidence back (which will be when you get to the end of this book!) before you go in and chat again.

The GIRL POWER Boys-as-Friends Checklist

☆ Be prepared if your mum and dad can't understand that a boy is just a mate and not a boyfriend.

☆ Don't be tempted to respond if any male geeks take the mickey. Keep the upper hand and simply say 'You're not worth the comment' and walk away.

☆ Boys can be as much fun as girls.

☆ Remember that boys tend to mature later than girls.

☆ There's no reason to assume that boys won't be sympathetic and thoughtful.

BOY FRIEND OR BOYFRIEND?

THERE is no magic age when girls start going out with boys. Some of your mates might have gone out with a boy for the first time when they were twelve or thirteen, others might not have a boyfriend by the time they are sixteen or more. You'll know when there is a boy that you fancy going out with – and it will happen the day that you meet him, no sooner and no later than that.

I don't fancy any of the boys in my school. They're just a bunch of morons who have farting competitions and talk about football all the time. What's wrong with me?

ABSOLUTELY NOTHING! You've just got more sense than to fancy one of those morons and much better things to do with your time than hang around telling them how clever and handsome they are (which is quite possibly what they'd like the girls to be doing).

You've got your own life to lead: things to discover, people to meet and places to go to. So don't worry about why you don't fancy any of them because it's quite obvious why you don't! There is nothing wrong with you – it's the boys who have got the problem and need to grow up.

The boys in my school are OK. But I still don't fancy one – what should I do?

IT DOESN'T MATTER if you don't fancy one. There is absolutely no need for you to rush into having a boyfriend. In fact, about the worst thing a girl can do is have a boyfriend for the sake of having one. Some girls go out with a boy just because all their friends have got boyfriends. So they put up with a bloke whose company they don't really enjoy and who they may not even fancy *just* so that they can say they've got a boyfriend. Sounds awful? Well, it is – and girls who put up with it don't have any girl power at all. So do absolutely nothing about the fact that you don't fancy any of the boys at school. You are already doing the right thing.

All my friends have got boyfriends and I haven't. One of my friends recently asked me why I hadn't got a boyfriend and when I said I hadn't met a boy I fancied she said I must be a lesbian.

FIRST OF ALL, exactly what has it got to do with your friend whether or not you've got a boyfriend? Isn't it your business rather than hers? And wouldn't she tell you to mind your own business if you asked her why she bothered to go out with her boyfriend? Secondly, just because you don't fancy every boy you meet doesn't make you a lesbian. Lesbians are women who find other women sexually attractive and are turned off by the idea of such a relationship with a man. So, if the reason why you haven't got a boyfriend is because you just don't fancy any of the boys you've met so far, there is no reason to assume that you will never fancy any boys.

Why not exercise your girl power and ask yourself why one of the people you count as a friend is being quite so narrow-minded and silly? Perhaps she isn't really a good mate after all.

I can't understand it. All my mates go on and on about how great-looking all these men in the soaps and singers are and I just don't get it at all. In fact, I think that some of the girls are really attractive and there's one girl pop star that I really fancy. Do you think I'm a lesbian?

FINDING another girl attractive does not automatically make a girl gay. Some girls find other girls sexually attractive and find the idea of fancying a boy in that way a real turn-off. Some girls find both boys and girls sexually attractive (that's technically called bisexuality). Most girls find some other girls interesting and stunning to look at but don't think about actually fancying them – they just think about their looks and their attitude.

The important thing to remember is that you should only be prepared to spend time with people you *like*, whatever their sex. No one should be made to think that they should be spending time with people they don't like just to be 'normal'. It takes most of us a while to work out exactly which way our sexual chemistry works. So, for the time being, try not to over-analyse life or your own sexuality – no matter how much pressure you feel from people. Believing in yourself and believing that you are the great person that you are, with a lot to offer the world, is real girl power. Don't let other people force you to find a category for you to fit into neatly at the earliest possible moment. And don't feel any pressure to prove anything to anyone – not even yourself! Don't let anyone make you believe that you are or aren't a lesbian if you're not sure yourself yet.

I really fancy a boy in my class.
How can I make him realise?

WELL, you could ask one of your friends to tell him but there can be drawbacks to this. For instance, your mate could make out that you are absolutely desperate to go out with him rather than just keen. Also, she could end up telling *his* friend to tell him rather than telling him direct – and the next thing you know, the whole school could find out who you fancy. So the best thing to do would be to exercise your girl power and tell him yourself. Here's the girl power guide to letting a boy know:

☆ Choose a time when he's on his own rather than with his friends.

☆ Don't go up and say something like, 'I really fancy you'. Instead, say something more subtle like, 'I wondered if you'd like to go to the school match/disco/a film with me on Saturday?'

☆ Don't start doing a hero-worship routine on him – you know, doing crazy things like going around with starry eyes and making deep sighs every time he goes past or constantly telling him how clever he is. Behaving like that will probably make him laugh at you. Worse will be if he is flattered by you being such a creep – do you really want to go out with a boy who's a big-head and who will expect you to massage his ego all the time?

☆ Accept it if he makes it clear that he doesn't want to go out with you. Of course you will be hurt and fed up about it but don't throw an emotional scene and start weeping in front of him. Be dignified and say 'OK, no problem'. Similarly, don't be rude to him and tell him to get lost.

☆ If he does turn you down, you are perfectly entitled to feel miserable and to have a good weep. In fact, indulge yourself in a night of total how-could-he-possibly-turn-down-someone-as-great-as-me ness. And then stop it. Put the whole thing down to one of your first experiences of asking a boy out, think about whether you'd approach the situation in the same way again or if you'd do it differently, and then get on with having a good time. Life is about the brilliant stuff that is happening now and in the future, not the unhappy stuff that happened in the past.

The GIRL POWER Boy Friend/ Boyfriend Checklist

☆ Don't expect boys *not* to be such good mates as girls.

☆ Boyfriends are not a necessity in life.

☆ Keep your dignity if a boy turns you down – and then go home and have a good sob-session, if that's what you want!

☆ If you fancy a bloke, ask him out.

☆ Being a lesbian is *different* to being heterosexual – but it doesn't make you *weird*.

☆ Being without a boyfriend and being happy is a zillion times better than being with a boyfriend and being unhappy.

82

KEEPING BOYS IN THEIR PLACE

HAVING boys as friends or boyfriends should be fun. However, despite what some girls may think and say, being with boys should not be the only goal in your life or even the only goal of your social life. So make sure you keep those boys in their place!

Bossy boys

Since I've had a boyfriend I don't have nearly as much time to spend with my friends. If I tell my boyfriend that I can't go out with him and I want to go somewhere with my friends, though, won't he go off me?

A DECENT boyfriend should respect the fact that you've got other good friends as well as him. And why should you ditch the friends you've had for yonks just because of a boyfriend you've only just started to go out with? Doesn't your boyfriend like to spend time with his own mates as well? In which case, of course he will understand that you need time to yourself and your friends because he can't expect you to sit at home on your own at the times that you aren't with him. If he doesn't understand that, and won't compromise or try, then he isn't a decent boyfriend and he isn't someone for you.

My boyfriend is always telling me that he doesn't like the clothes I wear and reckons I should be wearing all this stuff like his sister. He also thinks I should do the same exam choices as him so we will be in the same classes next year. But I don't like his sister's

**clothes and I won't do nearly so well in those subjects as
he will. If I don't try to do what he likes, though,
I'll probably lose him. And, anyway, perhaps
he's right about the clothes.**

OH YES, and who is in charge of your life then? You or him? You have to do what you want to do and not what he wants you to do. If you want to wear your gear then wear it – as well as studying the subjects that interest you and that you will do well at. If your boyfriend really cares about you, he will respect how you feel and what you want to do. He should be happy that you are doing things that make you feel good and happy. And you are *you* and proud of it. You don't need to be made into a clone of his sister or anyone else for that matter. If he wants a clone, tell him to go elsewhere.

**My boyfriend has asked me to sleep with him.
I really love him but I don't want to get involved with him
that way – at least not yet. But I'm worried that he will
ditch me if I don't sleep with him.**

ALTHOUGH you might not think it at the moment, the answer to this one is actually really simple: don't sleep with him if you don't want to. If he's a decent person he should accept it when you tell him that's how you feel and you can carry on as before. If he doesn't accept it and keeps putting pressure on you to sleep with him, then he simply isn't a decent bloke and you should tell him to get lost – but you knew that anyway, didn't you? Follow your girl power instincts and remember:

☆ No boy should only be interested in what you can do

behind the bike shed or between the sheets. Chances are, if you do give in to such pressure, he'll soon dump you anyway because he will have thought of you as a trophy.

☆ No boy is worth doing something that you don't want to do.

☆ No boy will become more interesting because you sleep with him.

☆ No boy you sleep with will make you more grown-up or more exciting than you were before you slept with him.

☆ Your friends couldn't care less whether you sleep with him or not (if they do, they're not your friends).

☆ You should never have unprotected sex. Unprotected sex can make you pregnant and put you at risk of sexual diseases which could threaten your health in the long term.

☆ Being a virgin is nothing to be embarrassed about. And remember that you are only going to lose it once – so, when the time comes, lose it on your own terms not someone else's.

☆ You are in charge of what you do with your body, not any man (however old they are).

☆ If a boy lies and tells the world that you've slept with him when you haven't, tell a good mate the truth and ask her to spread the real news. Then have a word with the scum that started all this hassle and tell him not to act so cheap and boast about something he could only dream of getting.

The GIRL POWER Boys-in-their-Place Checklist

☆ It's OK to have a boyfriend, but only if you like him.

☆ Boyfriends are OK if they treat you as equals.

☆ Boys aren't the superior sex – and experience or being older than you doesn't necessarily make their opinions any more valid.

⭐ Be in charge of yourself.

⭐ Do what *you* want to not what *he* wants.

⭐ Make the most of the world for yourself.

⭐ Have fun.

⭐ Drop him if he doesn't understand why any of the above points are important to you! (OK, so give him a chance if you think he might not realise how claustrophobic/bossy/annoying he is being. Explain how you feel and let him try to treat you properly. If he doesn't change, though, part company.)

6

Golden Oldies And Sophisticated Superiors

HOWEVER in control you are, there are always going to be people older than you who are, or at least think they are, more in control than you. It's a fact of life.

Now, some older people are OK – in fact they can be great and really supportive and friendly when you need advice about something. But other folks can be a complete pain – always in the way when you need some privacy (like your mum, who's likely to interrupt your phone call with the boy you recently met at a party and ask you, in a very loud voice, why you left your knickers on the floor in the bathroom) or when you are having fun (like your dad, when he thinks you should be tucked up with your hot-water bottle in your winceyettes in bed instead of watching 'E.R.'

You can't *beat* the golden oldies but then you probably don't want to *join* them either, do you? So, instead, it's probably a good idea to work out how a girl with power can live alongside them and get on with life her way.

HOW TO KEEP PARENTS AND OTHER RELATIVES UNDER CONTROL

IT MAY be hard to imagine but absolutely everyone has a mum or dad who is expert at sometimes saying totally embarrassing things – just like your own. In fact, your mum or dad complained about the same things that you moan about – only in respect of your grandparents all those years ago! So even though you think they all gang up together against you now, they all felt the same way about their own parents way back then.

How can I get my mum to switch off at parent and teacher meetings at my school? She always gets into a huddle with a teacher and says something stupid like 'Oh, she wants to be a fashion designer' to my PE teacher or 'Oh, she wants to study physics' to the head of science. I don't want to do either of those things!

DON'T worry too much because teachers have had hundreds of parents come up to them and tell them things that they soon learn aren't necessarily the truth. Mums and dads sometimes go overboard at parent and teacher meetings simply because they are dead proud of their little babies – even if they are now great big babies as big as them, with minds of their own. The thing is, mums remember comments their kids make, for many years. So, if you once mentioned, when you were nine, that you'd quite like to be a fashion designer and haven't since talked much about the fact that you want to be an airline pilot (or a bus driver or a Formula One racer or whatever it is you want to do), that is probably why she mentioned the fashion designer bit to your teacher. You see, no mum or dad would be happy to admit to a teacher that they weren't sure what you wanted to do because you hadn't told them or that you (and they) didn't understand the crummy subject that the particular teacher they are talking to teaches.

So, the way that girls with power cope with such a situation is by giving their parents some information (even if it is only a little incey-wincey bit) before the meeting starts. Here are the girls with power parent/teacher tactics:

☆ Have a quick chat with your parents the night before the meeting, or at least on your way to the meeting.

☆ Tell your mum and dad if there is a career that you are interested in and say which teacher you think it would be best to talk to about it.

☆ If you haven't the faintest idea what you want to do (and lots of people haven't, so don't feel remotely worried about it if you don't), tell your parents. Tell them that you want to speak to your careers teacher for more ideas.

☆ Tell your mum and dad if you know that you have fallen behind in a subject. Don't wait and let them find out from your teacher that you did so badly in chemistry that you managed to blow up the lab . . .

☆ Despite the chat you had, your parents may start telling a teacher that their subject is your favourite and that you want to study it to a higher level, when *you* know that you hate their subject and can't wait to get the chance to drop it fast! If they do, wait until you can *politely* interrupt and say something like, 'Oh I'm sorry, Mum, I think you've got confused with another subject.' That should give you the opportunity to get things straight. And, if necessary, go and see the teacher they blabbed to the next morning. Be as nice as nice can be and say you are so sorry that your parents got them confused with another teacher and that you hope that they didn't waste their time last night. Say, of course, that while you *are* interested in their subject, you know that you have a better chance of doing well in another subject and that it will be more use to you in the careers that you are interested in.

Both my parents go on at me about my clothes, the music I listen to, my friends, the programmes on telly that I watch – just everything. Why can't they leave me alone?

BECAUSE you are living in their house and they are responsible for you. Mums and dads always want to do the best for their kids and are worried that if things don't turn out to be super-perfect (albeit in their eyes) it will have been their fault because they didn't try hard enough. The bottom line is that you are living in your mum and dad's home – so what goes on in it is up to them really. What you have got to do is try to live alongside them without facing lots of aggro. What you need is:

The GIRL POWER Guide to Parents and Grandparents

☆ Don't deliberately do things that will get up their noses! If you know that they hate you to leave dead tea bags in the sink, or moan if you play your music too loud, or prefer to let your kid sister practise the piano without the telly on, don't do all those things – or at least try not to do them all the time.

⭐ Don't tell lies. OK, you've had a nightmare and done something stupid. Don't expect your parents not to find out about it – get real! They are parents and they have this in-built instinct to sniff out lies at a million metres! Come clean as soon as possible. Then, no matter how much and for how long they moan at you, you can say, quite truthfully and piously, 'Well at least I did the decent thing and told you about it.' Whatever it is you have done wrong, they would have to admit that you got that bit right!

⭐ See if you can have some space to call your own. Your parents need privacy from *you* just as much as you need privacy from *them* so they should understand! Make sure that they know you need to spend time each day in your own room so that you can study, chill out, listen to your music (with your headphones on if necessary), have your mates round for a chat, and just be yourself. If you have to share a room with a brother or sister, see if you can find a way to divide up the room so that you each have a bit to call your own.

⭐ Don't keep too many secrets. Sure there will be some things that you don't want to let on about (like the blokes in the soaps that you fancy) but don't worry about things on your own. If something is worrying you about a teacher, or if a friend is up to something that you think is bad news, don't keep it to yourself. The corny old saying that a problem shared is a problem halved is honestly true. If you find it hard to talk to your mum or dad, try talking to your gran or grandad about it – sometimes this is easier because they will remember times when your mum or dad got into similar situations as you. And at least some of the stories that they might tell you will be good for a laugh!

☆ Try not to be enemies with your parents. This doesn't mean that your mum has to be your best friend but it does mean that, if you don't spend your entire time fighting with her, when you do fall out with her it should be easier to resolve. The same goes for your dad.

☆ If you get into an argument with your parents, try to think twice before you say something in the heat of the moment that you will later regret. This is perhaps easier to say than to do and most adults could do with having a go at it too. But at least think about what you want to say about a situation if you think a fight is brewing.

☆ Try to see things from their point of view sometimes. How would you feel if *they* spent two hours in the bathroom every morning and used up all the hot water so that you couldn't wash your hair or get to school on time?

SOPHISTICATED SUPERIORS
WHO JUST SEEM UNTOUCHABLE

IF you aren't in the top year at your school, those dead cool senior students can sometimes seem just too sophisticated for words and a bit intimidating. So use your girl power to cope with them.

I've just left an all-girl school and started at a mixed one. It's full of really glamorous older girls and good-looking older boys. I feel like a boring nobody.

AND they felt the same when they started at the school too because they weren't the oldest students. Now they've had a whole year to get to know each other and get used to wearing their school uniform which they've adapted to make their own style. Meantime, you've been developing your girl power and have almost certainly got loads of interesting things to do and talk about – so you can't be boring. If you want to get more confidence in the things you wear, go back to chapter two, Your Image and check out the advice about your clothes again.

So what's the cool way to behave with older students?

IT'S COOL to behave as yourself because that is what you're best at.
Don't:

☆ Behave like a quiet little mouse who doesn't want to interrupt things. (Then they *will* think you are boring!)

☆ Be over-the-top, loud-mouthed and butt in with your own opinions all the time. (Then they will just think you are a self-opinionated show-off.)

☆ Cringe and fawn all over the seniors and tell them how clever they are all the time. (It's just the same as with boys you fancy: if they like *you* behaving like that, then *they* aren't worth liking!) With girl power you don't need to be a creep to impress people and get them to like you. And you don't need anyone's approval.

☆ Treat college like a fashion show. (They care about you not your clothes.)

Do:

☆ Join in with any school clubs. (It's a good way to make friends with the older kids.)

☆ Say hello to them if you bump into them in the corridors. (Then they will know you are not a mouse.)

☆ Speak to your teacher if you are being harassed or bullied by one of the senior students. (There is no point in your life being made miserable by a miserable person. Also, there is a good chance that this bully is known to be a bully and has done it to another younger student before.)

☆ Enjoy being there and being treated more like an adult.

TEACHERS AND HOW TO GET ON WITH THEM TO MAKE YOUR LIFE EASIER

THERE is no way you can avoid teachers in your life. And, just like other people, there are nice ones, nasty ones – and even good-looking ones!

Teacher troubles

My class teacher spends all her time picking on me and showing me up in front of the others. She's an old bag and I hate her . . . and I don't know what to do about it.

ONCE upon a time, all teachers were permanently strict, never smiled, and beat the students that weren't brilliant and didn't behave in an absolutely perfect manner all of the time. Now, thank goodness, life at school and college is a bit more relaxed and most teachers are OK – at least some of the time. In fact, some of them are even good fun and almost likeable. BUT, teachers are not saints and some of them find certain students difficult to handle. Are you certain you don't deserve some of the criticism she aims at you? OK, OK! So you don't deserve it. Do you have a grievance procedure at your school? If you do, you should be given the opportunity to go along to a teacher who has the particular role of acting as an arbitrator: you can go to him or her and explain what you think the teacher is doing and ask them to sort it out. Before you jump to the conclusion that all teachers will stand up for each other, remember that it is this teacher's job to sort out the problem, so they will have been chosen for their fairness and diplomacy (yes, some teachers do have both). They will want to help you and the teacher get on better. If your school doesn't have a teacher who has been selected to do this, go along to a teacher more senior to the one you have a problem with (like a year head or deputy head) and ask for their help.

I used to really enjoy my French lessons but now we've got a new teacher and I just don't understand what's going on half the time. I used to get good grades with my old teacher – not great, but OK ones. Now I'm so confused that I just can't do my homework properly – I just guess the answer. Is there anything I can do to get back to where I was?

THIS HAPPENS to lots of kids. You get on really well with a teacher and understand the way they do things so it makes you try hard at their class and you get good results. Then the teacher ups and goes off to another class and the new teacher you get has a different method of teaching that perhaps isn't quite so much fun or on your wavelength. And then you get confused or don't try so hard and your grades go down.

Now before you start sobbing in despair, remember that no teacher is going to want you to fail in their subject because, for a start, it doesn't look good for them either if you do. So what you need to do is have a word with the teacher and let them know you're finding their class difficult. This is a great girl power tactic because teachers will always admire a girl who can admit when things aren't perfect. Consequently they will probably have more time and patience for the problems you are having and should be more willing to help you get back on top of things. Once the teacher is on your side, ask them if they can spare you about fifteen minutes a week of extra tuition in their subject and perhaps (don't groan too loudly now) if they can give you some extra homework so that you can backtrack to the time when things started to get confusing. You can also ask the teacher to show you the answers that you should have got, so that you can start to understand where you went wrong.

I'm terrified of putting up my hand in class and asking my teacher to explain something. Won't everyone else think I'm a geek if I don't know the answer? Or, even worse, teacher's pet!

LISTEN, you are a girl with power and girls with power aren't perfect – they're realistic. You can not be expected to know everything in life and you'll really make it tough for yourself if you expect to. But girls with power want to know more about life. So why should you be embarrassed to say that you don't understand something or feel ashamed because you *do* know the answer to something? If the other kids in your class think people like you are geeks and pets, then they really are great geeks themselves, aren't they? The whole point about girl power is that you can stand up for yourself. Remember, short-term hassle or embarrassment at asking something is much better than the long-term hassle of pretending to know something you don't. Why sweat?

A good tip for asking a question (if you are worried about sounding like a pencil-case) might be to say to the teacher, 'Maybe I've missed something obvious here but I don't understand why . . .'

> **My maths teacher is really young and really, really, really good-looking. I know I'm in love with him and I'm sure that he loves me too. So why hasn't he asked me out?**

LUCKY YOU to have a young and good-looking maths teacher because it probably means you are trying so hard in maths that your grades have gone up! OK, so *you* are in love with *him* but can you really be certain that *he* is in love with *you*? Especially if you haven't been out with him – and perhaps haven't even spoken to him except for during your lesson? Maybe he smiles at you in the lesson – that is probably because your grades have improved . . . and he probably smiles at the rest of the students too . . . and he is probably smiling at you because you smiled at him. Maybe he touched your hand when he handed back your work file – but he did that to everyone else as well . . . or perhaps you deliberately brushed your hand against his. Perhaps your teacher is really nice to you – but then he's just a nice guy who's perfectly pleasant with everyone else in your class, isn't he?

This may sound hard but . . . wake up and get a grip! Sure, you are in love with your maths teacher – because you have a *crush* on him. Lots of girls (and boys for that matter) have crushes on teachers but it is extremely rare for a teacher to have a crush on a student. Sorry. Crushes should be fun – a chance to daydream about someone. But be careful not to take them seriously: crushes rarely end up in a relationship of an intimate kind. So, don't pester your teacher – in fact, try to sit at the back of the class and away from him for a while. And stop hanging around by the staffroom at lunch-time, trying to see him. You probably can't picture this at the moment but in a few weeks' or months' time you will most likely think that Mr Maths is actually not that good-looking after all and have gone off him.

But I've got a crush on one of the women teachers in my school – she's just great and I wish I could be like her. Does that mean I'm gay?

NOT NECESSARILY – but it does mean you've got a crush on the teacher, possibly because she has become a role model to you. Think about why you think she's great. Is it because she's attractive? Is it because she's got a brilliant hairstyle? Is it because she's a really good teacher or a great person? Or that she's got cool clothes and the type of figure you'd like to have? Don't worry about it. (And don't worry if you think you are gay either. See page 80.) Miss Crush is your female idol at the moment. There is no problem in you wanting to be like her – just as long as you don't try to look like her clone and copy her voice (you know, do a *Single White Female* number on her). And, just like Mr Maths, there's a fair chance that you'll soon find Miss Crush slightly less interesting to you than she is at the moment.

Strategies for Scholars with GIRL POWER

☆ Tackle any problem at school as soon as possible, *before* it gets out of hand and your grades suffer.

☆ Always tell the truth about the situation if you have made a complaint about someone or something. Don't exaggerate or lie – it undermines your case!

☆ Don't be rude or personal to, or about any teacher you are complaining about. You'll be less likely to be taken seriously.

☆ Don't swear at anyone. It isn't cool and doesn't reveal any girl power.

☆ Do your best to act on what you are told to do to improve matters – whether it's a teacher problem or one with your own studies.

☆ Keep out of the way of any teacher that you have a problem with as much as reasonably possible.

☆ If you think that you have genuinely tried to improve things but that the teacher hasn't, go back to the senior teacher and let them know what has happened.

☆ If you've got a problem with a particular subject, go to the library and borrow some books on the subject (you will be amazed to see some of the fantastic books they will have which won't be so boring as the textbook you have at school).

☆ Try borrowing some magazines on the subject (if it is French just see if they have got some French teen magazines) from the library.

☆ Watch the telly! There are some great programmes about all sorts of subjects, which make it a fun way to learn.

☆ If you have access to the Internet, check out any Web sites about your puzzling subject.

☆ If one of your mates is really good at a subject and you are not, see if they can help you catch up – just don't cheat and copy their essay because you're bound to be caught – and it won't help you to get better anyway.

DOCTOR AND DENTIST DILEMMAS

THE PROBLEM about going to the doctor or the dentist is usually because you only go to them when you've got a problem! Now, if you are a good girl and look after your teeth (see chapter two, Your Image) you should be visiting your dentist every six months anyway, even if there isn't anything wrong with your teeth. But you don't go to see the doctor just to say, 'Hi. I'm looking good and feeling great!' now do you? So you are probably going to say, 'Umm. I've got this bump,' or 'I've got these lousy periods,' or something like that, aren't you? And because you don't go to see a doctor and say that very often, you might be feeling a bit worried about how to handle the situation, perhaps?

My family has just moved to a new dental practice and I really hate the dentist who did my first check-up there. He said I needed some orthodontal work which he is going to be doing himself. I'll need to have frequent appointments, but I just didn't like the man. He gave me the creeps for some reason. What can I do about it?

100

IF you really don't like your dentist, for whatever reason, ask if you can change to another dentist at the practice. Tell the receptionist, 'I would prefer to have my treatment carried out by (then give the name of another dentist at the practice or just say "someone else") please. Can that be arranged?' You don't have to give a reason why but if they ask, just say something like, 'I'd just prefer to see someone else, thanks.' If for some reason they can't do that, you are perfectly entitled to take your teeth to another dentist. In fact, if there is only one dentist at the place, you'll have to do that anyway, won't you? Whatever you do, don't let this man stop you from going to see dentists completely. *Never* forget that you are the girl with the power and in control of the situation!

I get on absolutely fine with my dentist but she's just told me that I need to have some treatment (fillings and stuff) that will take a couple of appointments. I'm terrified!

FORGET all the horror stories that people may have told you in the past about their trips to the dentist – they will almost certainly have exaggerated any pain which they claim to have been involved. The most likely reasons for them to do this are firstly to make the story sound more dramatic and therefore more interesting than a plain old trip to the dentist, and secondly to make themselves out to be a bit of a hero who managed to live through and survive a large amount of pain.

With modern dentistry, pain is a thing of the past. Treatment is carried out using modern, speedy machinery so it happens in a flash. And anyway, you will be given a local anaesthetic in your gums so that you won't feel anything. In fact, some dentists even put a special tincture on your gums *before* they give you an anaesthetic so that you can't even feel the needle!

Remember that the dentist is there to make your teeth and gums better, not because they want to be some kind of dental torturer. They want to make sure that what they are doing doesn't hurt and that you will be happy to come back and see them again. Which, of course, you might not be likely to do if they hurt you! So don't suffer pain or rotting teeth because girls with pain are not girls with power. The pain is not going to go away on its own and, as you've now heard, a trip to the dentist will result in less, not more, pain. So be powerful and make that appointment *now*.

It's the doctor that worries me. I've got problems with my periods but I feel really embarrassed about talking about them with my doctor.

THE DAY that you go for your appointment, your doctor is likely to already have seen at least one girl or woman who has period problems, and is also likely to see at least one more after they have seen you as well. So you won't be talking to the doctor about something they don't deal with often – or that they are embarrassed about.

If you are worried about talking to a male doctor about girl stuff, you could consider going to see them with your mum or another female relative. After all, you must have talked to your mum or someone about your periods at some stage, haven't you? If that idea doesn't appeal to you either, you could consider having a word with the school nurse. Alternatively, you could find out if your doctor's surgery has got a nurse practitioner. A nurse practitioner is quite likely to be a woman and would be happy to make an appointment to see you to talk about your problem – in fact, if you need any further help or treatment, they may well be able to continue to treat you without having to refer you to someone else.

If there isn't a nurse or nurse practitioner at your doctor's surgery and it's a group practice, ask if you can see one of the female doctors. If there isn't a female at the practice you are registered at, make enquiries at your local library to see if they can tell you where a woman doctor practises in your area. There may also be a Youth Health Centre in your area where you can go for advice. Whatever you do, if you are under the age of eighteen, you should have a word with your mum and dad before you move away from the family doctor's practice.

Once you've made your appointment, don't worry about what they are going to do to you because they probably won't have to do anything to you at all! A doctor is most likely to ask you questions rather than do any poking and prodding. Therefore it's a good idea to have the answers at your fingertips so that you can feel in control. Questions might cover some of these areas:

☆ When was your last period?

☆ How long was your last period?

☆ Do you have a regular cycle for your periods? (Which means, do you have periods at regular intervals that each last about the same length of time? Don't worry if you aren't very regular because few women are until they have been having periods for a number of years.)

☆ Do you have period pains?

☆ When do your period pains start and finish?

☆ Do you get tender breasts?

☆ Are you on a diet?

☆ How much do you weigh?

☆ Do you suffer from headaches or any other aches and pains?

If the doctor needs to examine you, they will almost certainly do this with a nurse present. And (this may sound easier said than done) don't feel embarrassed about your body. Doctors have looked at so many bodies in various states of undress that they've seen all shapes and sizes – yours won't surprise them at all. Anyway, it is extremely unlikely that you will have more than a few centimetres of flesh on any part of your body exposed at any one time.

The doctor might ask to weigh you and she or he may also check your blood pressure using a pump which is attached with a sort of cuff around your upper arm (it doesn't hurt!). It is important for you to sort out any worries that you have about your periods because just putting up with problems and worrying away about them can wear you down and start to make you self-conscious about going out during your period.

DOCTOR, DOCTOR! HAVE YOU HEARD THE ONE ABOUT THE GIRL WITH POWER WHO KNOWS HOW TO HANDLE DOCTORS AND DENTISTS?

Here's what she'll do:

☆ Say, 'Excuse me, please stop that a moment,' if any dental treatment isn't pain-free. Tell them it hurts! It may be a hard time to exercise your girl power but it is one of the most important times!

☆ If you don't like a doctor or dentist, change to another one.

☆ If you need more than your own girl power, take someone else with you when you go for a check-up.

☆ Your health is important to you.

☆ Girls with power get things which are worrying them sorted rather than letting the problem get out of hand.

☆ Doctors and dentists aren't there to lecture you, they are there to help you. So don't let them dismiss you or rush the appointment without listening to you. Better still, before you go to the appointment, write down a list of the things you want to ask them about and take this into the appointment with you.

☆ If you don't trust what a doctor or dentist has said to you, arrange for an appointment with another one and ask for a second opinion.

7

Getting A Life

THERE'S an old saying that 'The world is your oyster' and when you get to your teens the golden oldies start muttering it to you at frequent intervals and then giving a deep sigh. What, you may well wonder, are they on about? Because if you think about it, an oyster is a fishy-smelling, cold, scratchy shell that clamps down on its contents. So are they telling you that life is going to be dead boring and that you're going to live in an atmosphere like a prison? Or are they actually telling you that your life could turn out to be like the thing that everyone hopes to find *inside* the oyster – a luscious, shiny pearl? To be honest, what they are really saying to you is that the answer is mostly up to you. If you go for it, you could end up pearly. If you don't, you'll stay inside the shell. Heavy stuff, eh? But definitely worth thinking about.

SCHOLASTIC CONSIDERATIONS

SCHOOL is only part of your life but it is a big part, that's going to help you get what you want in your future. So it is important that you get school organised properly so that you can make the best of it – and the best of yourself.

I used to be really organised about my homework and stuff but now that I'm doing exam courses I just seem to end up in a muddle all the time. Sometimes I even forget to do some of my coursework – and that's part of my exam material. If I don't get it sorted soon, I'll go down in my grades.

ONCE you get to the exam stage or pre-exam stage in life, it's important to make sure that you have got time allocated for doing revision, homework – and having a bit of fun! At some schools the teachers help the students to organise a study timetable which is a bit like the timetable you follow while you are in school but it's just the one you do at home. If your school hasn't done this, why not have a word with your form tutor or your year head and see if he or she can help you to work out a schedule of how to get everything done?

If there isn't anyone to help you try doing the following:

☆ Write down a list, day-by-day, of the subjects that you are likely to get for homework.

☆ On the nights when you don't get so much homework (dream on!) slot in some time for coursework.

☆ Stick this list up on your wall above the area where you usually study at home and tick each subject off as you do the work.

☆ Don't forget to put some slots on your list for things like reading magazines or books or watching the telly or for seeing your mates. It's important for you to have some fun in your life and fun helps to give you the energy you need to do all the studying as well! After all, that's what girl power is all about.

**But some nights I have so much homework
I don't have time to do anything else!**

IF that is the case, why not have a word with your form tutor? It could be that she or he can help you spread the load over the whole week by having a word with some of your subject teachers. It may be the case that not all the essays and things have to be in immediately so you can have a breather while you get on with other stuff. No teacher wants you to fail in their subject and they certainly won't want you to be stressed and unhappy. They will appreciate you showing your girl power and standing up for yourself when the chips are down; they should be happy to be realistic about what anyone can expect from you. Especially if you have been organised enough to show them the homework and coursework timetable that you've tried to work out for yourself!

The GIRL POWER Guide to Spicing up School Life

☆ Remember school is only one part of your life.
☆ Life is about having fun – and at least some of school should be fun too.
☆ When school is out, make time to get to grips with your homework as well as having time to go out with your mates.
☆ If you are getting bogged down with your work, seek help rather than getting deeper into a mess.

EXAM SUBJECTS, CAREER PROSPECTS AND OTHER SERIOUS STUFF THAT PEOPLE WILL KEEP BUGGING YOU ABOUT

OK. So it's up to you. You can have virtually anything you want in life which is pretty great really. Now you don't have to decide now, this very minute, what you want to do every day until the time of your retirement and beyond, and stick to it rigidly. But it is an idea to have a think about the sort of things you fancy doing because it is one way of helping you to make decisions about the subjects you want to take exams in. That way you can make sure that you actually *get* what you want rather than miss out on any chances because you didn't know about them until it was too late.

I haven't a clue what I want to do when I leave school – but everyone seems to expect me to! It's like there is all this pressure on me to say, 'I want to be a brain surgeon' or something that sounds really impressive. I'm just happy having fun at the moment and I don't want to have to think about exams.

YOU'RE RIGHT. Some people do get a bit worked up about careers and things. Especially parents, teachers and grandparents. But the trouble is, when you get to being about thirteen or so, you are going to have to face the fact that exam choices are very near. And the subjects that you choose to do now are going to be with you for at least two years – so it's best to use your girl power now and select the subjects that you want rather than leaving it to other people to force you into deciding.

By now you will have had enough time at school to have a very good idea of the subjects that you:

a are good at;

b enjoy;

c are useless at;

d loathe.

So sit down now and get yourself four pieces of paper. Mark one sheet **a**, the next one **b**, the third one **c**, and the last one **d** and write down on the sheets the subjects that apply to the above headings. Now, some of the subjects in list **a** will almost certainly be in your list **b** so that's a good start to giving you an idea of which exam subjects to opt for. But although it's unlikely that your lists **b** and **c** have much in common (are you some kind of sadist, girl?), there is still a possibility that a subject can crop up in your list **a** and still be in your list **d**. And it is these list **a** and **d** duplicates that can be a problem, because they are the sort of subjects that teachers and other golden oldies may give you a hard time about: 'How can you possibly give up theoretical engineering – you are *so* good at it?!' they will say. And because you have got girl power you can say, 'Because I don't enjoy it and really do enjoy quantum physics – so I'm going to do that instead!'

Once you have come up with a list of subjects which you think you would like to opt for, consider carefully whether they will, overall, give you and your brain a well-balanced 'diet' of subjects which offer you variety of subject matter and a mixture of essays, reading and practical work. Remember all work and no play gives a girl no power at all!

A visit to the school careers adviser may also be a good idea in helping you choose some subjects but only if you have already had some thoughts about what you might fancy doing as a career once school and stuff is over. If you have, a careers adviser may be able to let you know if there are some subjects that you simply *must* have taken exams in before they will consider you for future training or a job. If, like most people, you don't know what you want to do in life, try to keep a wide base of subjects that will allow you more choice later on.

The GIRL POWER Exam Strategy Checklist

☆ Don't worry about life! If you don't know what you want to do, you are not a failure.

☆ Don't be pressurised by someone (whether it's your parents or a teacher) into making a decision when you aren't ready to (but do remember that sometimes there will be deadlines you'll have to meet).

☆ Don't be bullied into taking a subject just because someone else says it is what you should do. If you aren't certain about it then don't commit yourself.

☆ Have a chat with some of the older students in your school about how they came to make a decision about what to do next.

☆ Take a large sheet of paper and a pen, make yourself a cup of coffee and settle down to a quiet afternoon's luxurious thinking of nothing but yourself. Divide the page into two columns and write down all the things you know you don't want to do in one column and all the things you quite fancy doing in the other column. Don't just write down things to do with jobs: write down things like, 'I want to go to America' or 'I don't want to go to Argentina'; things about celebs that you'd like to meet; that you would like to learn to drive, or speak another language, or train guide dogs for the blind, or learn to deep-sea dive, or . . . whatever you can think of. Take your time over doing this because it's your life that you are thinking of. When you've finished, you will have a unique picture of how you feel about things. You should have enjoyed doing it (which is the most important thing, when people around you are getting serious) – and you may even have come up with some exam subject ideas to select at the same time!

MONEY – SADLY AN IMPORTANT PART OF A GIRL'S LIFE

ONE WAY, but by no means the only way, to have fun is by spending money doing things or buying things. The problem with money though, is that you have to get hold of the cash in the first place. If you are incredibly lucky and your parents are millionaires, perhaps you get a load of pocket money donated to you every week. But, of course, we live in the real world, which means that the way to get money is to earn it and getting a part-time job while you are still at school is a good way to start.

Just the job!

Now that I'm old enough, I'd love to get a Saturday job to help me save up for clothes and things. But my parents won't hear of it and are refusing to let me go for one. What can I do?

WAIT one moment! Are you sure that you are old enough? There

112

are laws and regulations that have been established to make sure that teenagers aren't exploited or doing too much so that they can't cope:

⭐ If you are thirteen or fourteen, you can work a maximum of two hours on a weekday or Sunday and five hours on a Saturday.

⭐ If you are fifteen or over, the two-hour rule still applies to weekdays and Sundays but you can work up to eight hours on a Saturday.

But, getting back to your mum and dad, have you found out why your parents are against the idea of you getting a job? Was it because you found a job that you wanted to apply for in a place that your parents thought was unsuitable for some reason? If it was the location and the actual job itself that they disapproved of, then why not suggest to them that you look for something else?

Perhaps, though, your parents are against you getting a Saturday job, full stop? Again, if this is the case, then you need to find out why. A common reason for parents (and, indeed, some teachers) not liking their teenagers getting a part-time job is because they think that the job will take up too much of their time and stop them from doing well at their studies. So you could try persuading your parents that you will work every weekday evening at your schoolwork and even do some on Sundays so that you can have the whole of Saturday off from homework (because, let's get real, after a day working in a shop, or waiting at tables or serving up fish and chips, you are not going to be in the mood to tackle a history essay or a light spot of revision for physics). You could also suggest that you give the Saturday job a try and if you fall back in your schoolwork you will reconsider the job. The problem with both of these tactics is that you are going to have to be prepared to fulfil them! If you don't get to grips with balancing the job without compromising your studies then you will be sunk in your parents' eyes – and you'll probably have to give up the job. So, really, it's up to you to exercise your girl power.

My parents are fine about me having a Saturday job, I just don't know how to get one!

WELL for a start you should think about the things that you like doing or hate doing that you listed on page 111. Then you can see if any of them are compatible with a part-time job. Think about looking for work in:

☆ A local shop. It could be the corner shop or part of a national chain of stores. The work could be for Saturdays only or for an evening or early morning during the week – in fact, a corner shop or newsagent is quite likely to want people who work odd hours during the week.

☆ A local restaurant or fast food place. You could work behind the counter serving up the food, as a waitress or do washing-up.

☆ The library. Some libraries need unqualified library assistants to help out on Saturdays.

☆ In a cinema. This would be either selling the tickets or working as an usherette.

☆ A local supermarket. There are many different jobs in supermarkets: you could work at the checkout, at the newsagent kiosk, in the stockroom, in the bakery, stacking shelves or perhaps as a packer and carrier.

You could also think of setting yourself up in work as a baby-sitter (the law says you have to be at least fourteen before you can be responsible enough to do this), a car washer, a cleaner or a gardener.

I fancy the idea of getting myself some regular baby-sitting. What's the best way to go about it?

YOU need to be careful for a start, because you don't want your telephone number to fall into the hands of strange people, do you? If you want to do baby-sitting, ask the parents of any young children that you know if they need a sitter. In turn, ask them to mention you to their friends. Or place a card with your details on the notice-board of your local nursery school or child health clinic. (Similarly, if you wanted to set up a car-washing business, you could look for custom amongst your parents, and aunts and uncles and their friends. Do the same if you fancy working as a cleaner or someone who can tidy up the leaves in the garden.)

If you do set yourself up in business, remember to follow these golden rules:

☆ Never work for someone you don't know – or at least make sure that someone you know knows them well.

☆ Never go to work for someone at their house without telling your parents, or another adult, exactly where you are going and when you expect to be back.

☆ Agree a fee for the work you are going to do *before* you start working.

☆ Tell them in advance that you expect to be paid in cash as soon as the work is complete.

☆ If you are baby-sitting or doing an evening shift in a restaurant or fast food place, work out in advance how you are going to get home, especially if it is late at night.

EXAM FAILURE – RESIT OR RETHINK?

THERE isn't a single person in the world who hasn't failed at something. Even a genius can be a lousy cook or fail their driving test. But, even if you were expecting a poor result, being given direct proof that you have failed your mocks or end-of-year exams or just haven't done as well as you originally hoped to do, isn't a whole heap of fun. In fact, exam failure or disappointment leads to the 3Ds: 1. **Despair** (when you realise what you haven't got); 2. **Decision** (when you have to decide what you can or want to do about it) and 3. **Doing** something about it (which is when you have to get on with what you have decided to do!).

I've just got my exam results and some of the grades are what I was expecting but others are much lower. I've even failed one of them so I don't think I will be able to do the exam choices I originally wanted to.

IT'S EASY to give up on everything when you get a disappointing result – but don't! First of all you should arrange to go to see the teachers of the subjects that you were hoping to study to find out if there is any way you can still start their exam courses. This will take some girl power but most teachers will be impressed if you care enough to want to do something about confronting your failure or disappointment. If you really want to carry on with a subject and think that your result could put the mockers on doing so, try asking the teacher if you can sit another exam as soon as possible. Remember that this will mean extra work for your teacher because they will have to set another paper for you (you didn't expect them to let you resit the previous one, did you?!) so don't go in demanding – go in asking politely. If you do get the chance to try again, make sure that you give yourself the best possible chance to pass or at least get a better result. If you can't convince yourself that you can do something well, you almost certainly won't let yourself do well at it and that is far too high a hurdle to make yourself jump. If you don't pass second or third time around, at least you will know that you gave it all you had.

If you have failed in something, try not to give yourself a really hard time. No one can be good at everything and failing at one thing is not the end of the world. Girl power is all about knowing what you are bad at (as well as knowing what all your good things are) and if, despite your best efforts, you can't crack a subject, try to accept that you and it aren't suited. Be positive – work as hard as you can for as long as you can (or have to) at a subject before you decide to drop it. Even if you weren't brilliant at it, you will have learned *something* from it.

The GIRL POWER Exam Failure Strategy

☆ Don't panic. If you expected to do well, you will have been shaken up by the failure. Keep it in perspective and remind yourself that you can try again.

☆ Don't just sit and mope about failing.

☆ Failure doesn't mean that your brains have melted overnight. Work out if you failed because you just didn't do the revision (this will be easy . . .).

☆ Remember that we can't all be geniuses.

☆ Talk to your subject teacher and ask their advice on whether you have any hope of passing again in the near future.

117

☆ If you didn't understand something in the exam or the lessons, take this opportunity to speak to your teacher about it.

GET STREETWISE

NO GIRL has girl power unless she is streetwise. In other words, a girl has power if she can look after herself when she's out and about on her own or with her mates.

I can look after myself all right – but my mum reckons I can't get the bus home from school on my own. It makes me feel a right baby.

THERE CAN, of course, be some advantages in being picked up from school by your mum or dad, especially if it is cold and raining and they are collecting you in a car. But, other than that, going home with your mates on the bus just has to be a lot more interesting.

Perhaps you can enlist the help of your teachers at school to try to persuade your parents that you are a big, girl-powered girl now? Lots of schools have guidelines for parents and pupils about travel safety. Your school may be lucky enough to have a school bus service (most likely if you live in a rural area) or they may suggest that those pupils over a certain age are responsible enough to travel on the public bus service on their own – say after the age of about twelve. If you come into this category your parents will also want to think about how far you have to walk from the bus stop to your home, after you have got off the bus. It's probably not that far but you will need to convince your parents that you won't dawdle on the walk and you'll come straight back or that you and your mates will stick together. OK, OK, so this all sounds a bit 'Yes miss, no miss'. But, if you co-operate with Mum and Dad now, they will co-operate with you.

The bad news is that if you have to consider getting a train rather than a bus, lots of schools these days don't suggest that teenagers travel on their own until they are about fourteen. Bad luck.

The GIRL POWER Streetwise Strategy

☆ If you are going out, whether it's night or day, tell someone where you are going and when you think you will be back. (This doesn't mean that you don't have any privacy – it's just so that if you don't come back when you said you would, people know if they need to start getting worried about you.)

☆ Think about how you are going to get to the place and how you are going to get back *before* you set out for your journey.

☆ If someone offers you drugs or a drink that is already poured into a glass *refuse it*. The reason why you should turn down the drugs is obvious so let's not insult your intelligence by explaining it here. You may think that refusing the drink is stupid – but how do you know that the glass of what looks like orange juice hasn't got vodka or gin in it? Or that the glass of Coke hasn't been spiked with something much stronger that will actually make you feel quite ill? Or has perhaps had some drug put into it?

☆ Don't get legless. If you are paralytic, will you honestly be having fun? And will you be able to remember the night before, the morning after? And will you be safe? If you are drunk you won't be in control – and you certainly won't be a girl with power.

☆ Never go anywhere or do anything where you'll be vulnerable. Girl power doesn't make you invincible, it means that you don't get into situations you can't control.

☆ If anyone is hassling you or pushing you into something you don't want to do, say NO. Don't be afraid to be rude or forceful – there are times when being a 'nice girl' isn't appropriate. Your safety and feelings are far more important than the feelings of someone who's trying to push you around.

☆ Don't go out without enough money to get home again by public transport.

☆ Always have enough change to make a phone call from a public telephone or carry a phonecard with you.

☆ If you are out and a man (or a woman, for that matter) that you don't know offers you a lift home *don't accept it*, however nice they are.

☆ If someone offers a lift home to one of your friends *tell her (or him) not to accept it*.

☆ If you are with one of your older mates or one of your mates' older sisters or brothers and they are driving you home in their car and you think they have been boozing then refuse to get in the car with them. (It goes without saying that drinking and driving don't go together.) If that means that you will be stranded on your own, then call your parents immediately rather than try to return home by public transport if it is late.

☆ If you are stranded somewhere and need to get home, only travel in a licenced taxi. You will know if the cab is licensed because it will have a taxi licence plate displayed on the back of the vehicle (separate to the number plate). Tell the driver that you don't have the fare to get you home but that your parents will pay as soon as you get there.

☆ If a man wanders up to you and says that he's a minicab driver and would you like a lift, *refuse the offer.*

☆ Carry the phone number of a reputable minicab company with you when you go out.

☆ If you phone for a minicab when you are out, ask for a booking number or the name of the driver who is going to collect you. When the cab arrives, ask the driver what his name or the booking number is. If he can't provide the information, don't get in the car because he may just be a man who is cruising the streets looking for girls to pick up.

8

Going For It With Girl Power

RIGHT THEN, so now we've got this far, you're well on the way to understanding what girl power is all about. Hopefully you've discovered that girl power is:

☆ Something that you've already got.

☆ Something that you can get even more of if you try.

☆ Something that you can flaunt to your advantage.

☆ Something you can use to get the best for yourself.

GIRL POWER is all about believing in yourself. It's all about you realising you have great potential and that you can do what you want to do – when you want to do it. Girl power is about using the best things about yourself and making the not-so-good things better. Girl power is about actually *doing* what you want to do, rather than just thinking and talking about it. Girl power is about getting a life and getting on with it. Girl power is about having fun and having a good time.

The GIRL POWER Ultimate Checklist

☆ Look after your friends and they will look after you.

☆ If your friends don't look after you, consider whether they really are your friends.

☆ Having a boyfriend isn't everything.

☆ Not having a boyfriend is certainly not the end of the world.

☆ Be yourself.

☆ Enjoy yourself.

☆ If you aren't enjoying yourself, do something about it.

☆ Don't expect the world to arrive at your doormat – go out and explore it.

☆ Remember that school doesn't last for ever.

☆ Remember that at least some of school should be fun.

☆ Not knowing what you want to do doesn't mean that you will end up doing nothing.

☆ Remember that you are in control.

☆ Don't do something just because someone tells you to.

☆ Sort problems straight away.

☆ Never be afraid or too proud to apologise when you're wrong.

☆ Everyone has bad days – if you feel you've dealt with a situation badly, don't worry. Just pick your girl power back up and keep battling.

☆ Ask for advice if you think you need it.

☆ Never be worried or intimidated about expressing your own opinions.

☆ Remember that it is OK to change your mind.

☆ Your opinions can be different from other people's.

☆ Golden oldies used to be young and beautiful once.

☆ You are young and beautiful now.

☆ Don't be tempted to do things just to impress people.

☆ Don't let people dismiss you or get away with not giving you enough time – the time that you need.

☆ Your best image is probably the one you feel comfortable with.

☆ There is nothing to be ashamed of if you don't know or understand about something.

☆ If you don't know something, find out about it.

☆ Don't tell fibs too often.

☆ Don't keep too many secrets.

☆ If you do keep secrets, remember which ones you've kept so that you don't get yourself into trouble.

☆ Girls with power aren't aggressive, they are assertive.

☆ Being assertive is not being rude.

☆ Get yourself sorted and you can set about sorting the world to your liking.

☆ When you face a problem, step back and think. Use your girl power to approach the problem in a way which will get results: be practical, calm and flexible.

☆ Compromise can sometimes be better than an unresolved argument.

☆ Don't get stuck in a rut! If you think you've started on the wrong course, stop, think, and then set out to sort things so that you can start all over again.

☆ **HAVE FUN!** ☆

Girl Power

Get it!

Flaunt it!

Use it!

INDEX

If you would like more information about books available
from Piccadilly Press and how to order them, please contact
us at:

Piccadilly Press Ltd
5 Castle Road
London
NW1 8PR

Fax: 0171 267 4493